PRINTMAKING

A CONTEMPORARY PERSPECTIVE

PAUL COLDWELL

black dog publishing
london uk

CONTENTS

INTROD

UCTION

The history and development of printmaking is inextricably linked to the spread of ideas and records the changing way the world has been perceived by artists. Prints provide a mirror, reflecting the artist's engagement with technology however simple or complex, to produce multiple images that enter culture and circulate, finding their way into a variety of spaces and acting like an international currency, crossing boundaries, states and time.

The concept of a matrix from which multiple images can be printed, is still, I believe, a revolutionary one and one of the foundations of a sophisticated culture. From the first prints that were directly rubbed from woodblocks, to the four-colour offset presses that print anything from artworks to our books and periodicals and now into the digital age where an image file might be sent electronically across the world in seconds, the principle of dissemination and communication remains the same. This book aims to give a broad overview of the developments that have shaped this history of printmaking and to reflect on how the contemporary artist may work with these earlier analogue technologies in conjunction with and parallel to cutting edge digital developments.

Printmaking's history has been driven by three fundamental imperatives. First, to communicate to a wider audience through the capacity of print to produce multiple images. Secondly, to engage in the particular qualities that each process offers in order to expand the artist's expressive language and, thirdly, to respond to commercial necessities and opportunities. It is possible I believe to view all prints in terms of how they address these imperatives.

With these ideas in mind, I will look back at the history of printmaking to consider the principal developments that have signposted this history and, then, consider the contemporary situation and how artists are responding to new opportunities and technologies. For many artists the way in which new and old technologies compete in the contemporary scene has made for a dynamic exchange. Artists have at their disposal past techniques alongside digital technology, from which to select and integrate into their practice. While a number of artists at any time have drawn inspiration from the latest technology, whether this is, for example, the advent of lithography in the nineteenth century or laser-cuts in the twenty-first, others have been content to work within existing traditions. Both have resulted in prints of outstanding quality and refinement.

A BRIEF HISTORY OF PRINTMAKING PROCESSES

RELIEF PRINT

Relief print was the earliest form of printing and can be traced back to China in the seventh century with woodblock images, inked and then stamped on to paper in much the same way as a rubber stamp is used now. This method was gradually replaced by a rubbing method, which gave greater control and a more refined finish. Initially these prints were focused on the word and reproduced religious texts, however by the eighth century, in such manuscripts as the *Diamond Sutra*, images were incorporated alongside the text.

In Europe, the discovery of paper manufacturing in the thirteenth century provided the catalyst for the growth and spread of the printed image. The early woodcuts were initially rather crude, small black and white graphic images, depicting religious stories to a widely illiterate audience, which were sold at fairs or festivals, much like tourist souvenirs are today. They were generally simple line drawings, which had been translated into woodcuts to illustrate a story, with little attempt at shading or subtlety, they were ideal for printing alongside type.

Artists began to see the medium as offering something particular and not as a means to merely reproducing simple motifs. The German artist Albrecht Dürer was able to see within this simple technology its potential as an expressive tool way beyond the imaginings of his contemporaries. While the tradition had been to trace a drawing on to a woodblock before cutting, Dürer drew directly on to the block, (usually pearwood because of its tight structure) and oversaw the cutting of the drawing by skilled block cutters. This simple innovation brought the artist in to closer contact with the resulting print. It is easy to overlook the skill involved in these prints, with their lines appearing so fluid. The black printed line is the surface of the wood, the white areas having been cut away. The artist would also have to contend with the fact that the final image when printed would be mirror-reversed. Dürer's prints set new standards in both skill and complexity and were sold as both single complete images, as well as in bound form. In, for example, *Four Horsemen of the Apocalypse*,

ALBRECHT DÜRER, *Four Horsemen of the Apocalypse*, circa 1497–1498.
Woodcut, 39 x 28 cm.

circa 1497–1498, a print considered large at the time measuring 39 x 28 cm, Dürer produces not only a masterpiece of the craft but also one of the most enduring images of any period. Dürer's prints are complex and complete pictures in miniature demonstrating the inventiveness possible within the medium. The rendering of form, surface and texture belies the fact that the image is executed simply through line, the parallel lines of the sky not only reading as 'colour' against the white clouds but also creating movement across the whole surface. As Heinrich Wölfflin has commented, "German art up to then has nothing that can be compared to this effect of movement. Dürer brought the four figures, who appear in the text one after the other and had never before been shown as one group, closely together."[1]

The woodcut process was reliant on skilled cutters, placing a distance between the artist and the final work. In Europe, the woodcut was superseded by metal engraving, which enabled the artist to draw directly on to the plate. In Asia, however, the woodcut print had an extended history as the dominant print process with the later development of colour adding to its attraction. In China, colour printing was already commonplace in the late fifteenth century but it was in Japan, in the seventeenth century that this form of printing reached a pinnacle with the *ukiyo-e* or "floating world" woodcuts. In these multiple block prints, every aspect of contemporary life is celebrated in beautifully composed images published in a variety of formats, as individual prints, albums and books. RA Crighton in his introduction to The Floating World Exhibition at the Royal Academy divides these prints within five categories according to subject, Kabuki Theatre, Beautiful Women, Landscapes and Views, Nature and Heroes and Heroines.[2] But these prints also represent a clear example of the relationship of the print to commerce and industry. The artist would be commissioned to make an image, which would then be pasted on to the key block, and the drawing, again, would be cut by skilled block cutters. Colour notes would be provided for guidance, which when printed together with the master block in a specified order, resulted in the finished multicolour print. Each block added to the cost of production so there was an incentive in designing the prints with an economical use of colour. These prints were in great demand to satisfy the taste of a burgeoning middle class. The collaboration of publisher, artist, and craftsman as a means of producing prints is a model that continues today. Blocks would be sold on to other publishers and it was not uncommon for later editions to omit colours for the sake of economy. "There was no fixed size to an edition, blocks changed hands from publisher to publisher, and colour schemes vary considerably. Damaged blocks would often be recut, involving small changes in the image...."[3]

Three artists of particular distinction were Kitagawa Utamaro, Utagawa Hiroshige and Katsushika Hokusai. Utamaro produced serenely beautiful images of women, with a delicacy of colour and intricate compositions rendering transparency and fabrics to great effect. Some of these prints were portraits of celebrities or courtesans, and were appropriately revealing in the graphic possibilities of how they represented flowing hair, or the pattern of a kimono against pale skin. Some of Utamaro's best-known prints were erotic in nature, concealing explicit detail within an overall rhythmic design.

Hokusai and Hiroshige by comparison were best known for their landscapes. Hiroshige's epic series *The Fifty-three Stations of the Tokaido*, 1831–1834, traced the journey along the eastern sea road, connecting Edo with Kyoto. He produced a print for each of the staging posts along the road, providing an almost cinematic impression of the journey. The series proved to be an instant commercial success. Similarly, but with quite a different graphic style, Hokusai produced his series *Thirty-six Views of Mount Fuji*, circa 1831, which included *The Great Wave off Kanagawa*. This print, with its daring and inventive graphic realisation of a wave breaking, has become one of the most recognised single images from this period and has had an enduring influence, particularly evidenced in contemporary graphic novels.

Whilst in Asia, the end grain of the wood provided the surface to print from, giving sharp clear definition and detail, in Europe Paul Gauguin and the Norwegian artist Edvard Munch, amongst others, used the plank or cross-grain as a vehicle for a more gestural expressive mark-making. Nowhere is this more apparent than in Munch's *The Kiss*, 1897, where the image printed from the raised grain of the wood forms the brooding background to the lovers embrace. The two lovers have been cut out of the block, inked separately before being put back together like a jigsaw, prior to printing. This simple method provided Munch with endless possibilities for colour variations without any of the problems associated with multiblock registration. In these prints there is an economy and practical urgency that ties the image into the method of its making in almost perfect synchronicity. The degree of abstraction, experimentation and emphasis on simple but expressive colour combinations has made Munch's prints influential to a very wide range of contemporary printmakers.

The German artists, known as Die Brücke, considered the woodcut as the perfect vehicle for expressing raw emotions. Their prints were marked by a disregard for conventions of taste and refinement and found in the physical act of cutting and in the resistance of the wood, a metaphor for their primitive,

top: KITAGAWA UTAMARO, *Lovers in an upstairs room*, from *Uta makura* (*Poem of the Pillow*), 1788.
Woodblock print, 25.5 x 37 cm.

bottom: KATSUSHIKA HOKUSAI, *In the Hollow of a Wave off the Coast at Kanagawa; 'The Great Wave'* from *Thirty-six Views of Mount Fuji*, 1830–1831.
Woodblock print, 26 x 37 cm.

ERNST LUDWIG KIRCHNER, *Dancer with Raised Skirt*, from the portfolio *Brücke*, 1910.
Woodcut from a portfolio of two woodcuts, one drypoint, and one woodcut cover, 25 x 34.5 cm.

violent vision. Ernst Ludwig Kirchner's prints are a good example and illustrate how the whole block is used for dramatic effect. The image is conceived in terms of positive and negative shapes, while the complete design intuitively responds to the shape of the overall wooden block, making a feature of its irregular form.

Pablo Picasso, as with all his approaches to printmaking, developed relief prints in an individual and inventive way. Rather than wood, Picasso predominantly used linoleum for its ease of cutting and capacity to render a fluid line, and, through this material, he produced some of his finest and most poetic graphic works. Most significantly, he developed the process of reductive cutting, which involved printing the edition, colour by colour, from a single block, cutting away the linoleum progressively until only the final colour remained. This high-risk technique, sometimes referred to as "sudden death" was unforgiving, as any mistake would render the whole edition ruined. In *Still Life with Glass under the Lamp*, 1962, Picasso performs a *tour de force* demonstrating just how complex an image he could make from this process without inhibiting either the spontaneity or speed of his decision-making.

In the UK in the 1950s, Michael Rothenstein, an artist for whom printmaking was his principal form of expression, extended the vocabulary of relief printing with almost missionary zeal to include all manner of surfaces, from crushed cans to flotsam timber—in fact, using any surface from which an impression could be pulled. He challenged the notion that relief printing was a narrow process with its own strict rules and tools, giving his prints a great freedom, exuberance and richness of mark.

In contrast, the Polish artist Jerzy Panek, in his simple line woodcuts, dramatically cuts away to create linear prints depicting figures and animals, where very little of the original block remains. Panek's work is reminiscent of woodcut's folk tradition and also serves as a reminder that printmaking is still highly valued within Eastern Europe. This tradition is further evidenced in Georg Baselitz's large-format woodcuts and linocuts, characterised by their expressive cutting, hand-printing, and seemingly crude registration without regard for polite conventions. Often measuring over two metres in height, and with the motif drawn upside down, these prints are the embodiment of a confrontation between the artist and his material and a refusal to be confined

PABLO PICASSO, *Still Life with Glass under the Lamp*, 1962 (published 1963).
Linoleum cut, printed in colour, 62 x 75 cm. Digital image: The Museum of Modern Art, New York/Scala, Florence. © Succession Picasso/DACS 2009.

MICHAEL ROTHENSTEIN, *Bird and Sun*, 1956–1957.
Signed colour linocut, 38.5 x 58 cm. Courtesy Rothenstein Estate and Goldmark Art.

GEORG BASELITZ, *Eagle*, 1981.
Woodcut printed in black on offset paper, 65 x 50 cm. © Georg Baselitz.

THOMAS KILPPER, *The Ring*, London 2000, a South London Gallery project.
(clockwise from top) Woodcut on fabric, 400 m^2; View of the floor/matrix; The artist carving the parquet floor with a power router. Photos by Marcus Leith (courtesy Tate Gallery) and Jan Jacob Hofmann. Courtesy the artist.

top: ALBRECHT DÜRER, *St Jerome in His Study*, 1514.
Copperplate engraving, 25 x 19 cm.
bottom: ALBRECHT DÜRER, *Melancolia I*, 1514.
Engraving, 24 x 18.5 cm.

by traditional conventions." Baselitz has succeeded in incorporating the motif, even a series of motifs, into a picture without it becoming illustrative, narrative or anecdotal."[4]

A contemporary of Baselitz, Anselm Kiefer, himself a student of Joseph Beuys, has used woodcut to produce monumental images to confront ideas of German history. With many individual sheets pasted together, and then worked on with oil, shellac and other materials, these woodcuts have the physicality of ancient manuscripts. Indeed, he has also incorporated his prints and photographs into monumental books forming complete libraries. With Kiefer and Baselitz there is, particularly through their prints, a clear sense of connecting with the tradition of German Expressionism in the direct mark, emotive colour and uncompromising imagery. However, their greater importance within printmaking lies in their commitment to producing major works through the medium, both in terms of scale and ambition, to be seen as equals alongside their work in painting and sculpture.

One aspect of the continuing popularity of relief print lies in the fact that the artist can work at a large scale, relatively cheaply—the artist as scavenger, plundering skips and building sites for potential surfaces, not dependent or restricted by needing a press. An extreme contemporary example is Thomas Kilpper who, in 2000, spent months on a project entitled *The Ring* in which he took the parquet flooring of an abandoned office building near Tate Modern as his woodblock. Working on his knees with industrial tools and images projected down on to the floor as guides, Kilpper proceeded to use the whole floor area to make a single huge print, 400 metres square, which was then displayed, hung from the windows of the building as a banner. The printing was executed with the aid of a large adapted garden roller while the cut floor itself provided the venue for the private view where individual sections of the print were suspended from the ceiling. Here is print as installation, performance and public art, far removed from the sceptic's view of print as a being a commercial, safe, polite enterprise.

INTAGLIO

In the fifteenth century, while woodcuts functioned very well in conjunction with type, as an expressive medium it required great skill on behalf of the block cutters to translate the artist's drawing. There was a gap therefore between the artist's original drawing and the realised print, with the artist dependent on the cutter to interpret his work. By the mid-fifteenth century, the method of engraving into metal plates was developed both in Italy and Germany. Engraving gave artists a more immediate engagement with print, enabling the artist to work directly on the plate without necessarily having to have it translated by a craftsman. Engraving also had other advantages, the engraved lines printing positive as apposed to woodcut, where line had to be isolated. Furthermore, the burin used as the drawing tool in engraving gave the artist a tonal range depending on the depth of the incised line. Together, these qualities represented a dramatic refinement and offered the artist the possibility of drawing soft as well as hard forms. Martin Schongauer was one of the first artists to realise and capitalise on this new process and is attributed with the development of cross-hatching to suggest volume and tone.

The sophistication possible through this process is further evidenced and taken a degree further in the work of Dürer, who, as previously mentioned, had taken woodcut to a new level of sophistication. Similarly, with engraving, he was able to transform the medium and in works such as *St Jerome in his Study*, 1514, and *Melancholia*, 1514, he created images of remarkable sensitivity and realism, with an extraordinary range of surfaces, amplifying the softness of skin against cloth, stone against wood, with a subtlety previously unrealised in his graphic

top: JACQUES CALLOT, *The Hanging* from *The Miseries of War*, 1633.
Engraving by Israel Henriet, 8 x 18.5 cm.
bottom: HERCULES SEGHERS, *The Town with the Four Towers*, circa 1631.
Etching and drypoint, 20 x 32.5 cm.

Israel ex. Cum Priuil. Reg.
A la fin ces Voleurs infames et perdus ,
Comme fruits malheureux a cet arbre pendus
Monstrent bien que le crime (horrible et noire engeance)
Est luy mesme instrument de honte et de vengeance ,
Et que cest le Destin des hommes vicieux
Desprouuer tost ou tard la iustice des Cieux . 11

REMBRANDT VAN RIJN, The *Three Crosses*, State III, 1653.
Drypoint, 38.5 x 45 cm.

REMBRANDT VAN RIJN, The *Three Crosses*, State IV (lightly inked), 1653.
Drypoint, 38.5 x 45 cm.

work. Dürer engraved his own plates, allowing for a direct engagement with the whole process, his prints having an intensity and emotional charge that would have been impossible without such an intimate connection through the drawing.

But whilst engraving extended the graphic language from woodcut, one disadvantage was that the engraved plate could not withstand large numbers of printings, the plate quickly wearing down and therefore producing subsequently less rich impressions. The development of etching was dramatic for two reasons. First, it offered the artist a fluid means of drawing without requiring any particular craft skills and secondly, the process allowed for a greater number of impressions to be pulled from each plate. This made commercial sense and, as acids for etching the plates became more reliable and available, etching began to replace engraving as the preferred medium. A further attraction of the new process was that, in engraving, the burin tool was difficult to control—it required the artist to push the tool through the metal, physically making a groove in the plate. Etching, however, simply required the artist to draw through a wax ground and the depth of the line was determined through a combination of the strength of the acid and the length of time the plate was immersed.

Etching developed out of the crafts of decorating armour and jewellery before being taken up by artists as a medium. The French artist Jacques Callot, 1592–1635, who trained as a goldsmith, showed how delicate this new process could be in *The Hanging*, 1633, from the *Miseries and Misfortunes of War* measuring a mere 8 x 18.5 cm, yet packed with detail and incident, a widescreen vision in miniature. The *Miseries and Misfortunes of War* is also a good example of the way print could be used for political ends, challenging the establishment and speaking on behalf of the oppressed, the suffering peasant and soldier. "These are amongst the earliest examples of the print used essentially to communicate to as wide (and probably as unsuspecting) a public as possible the effect of the ravages of war, the moral issues, social conditions and political evils then prevailing."[5]

While Callot's prints can be seen as a development of the engraved line, Hercules Seghers, circa 1589–1638, discovered that etching opened up particular and distinct possibilities that were impossible through engraving. Seghers working within the Dutch landscape tradition, created imaginary landscapes using experimental techniques and deeply bitten lines. Rather than seek to make multiple copies, each print of Seghers' was unique, inked and coloured differently. This painterly approach to etching was an inspiration for, perhaps the greatest etcher ever, Rembrandt van Rijn.

Rembrandt approached etching not in terms of engraving as many of his predecessors, but as a distinct medium with its own syntax and it was largely due to his prints that he established an international reputation. He was visionary in realising how spontaneous etching could be, his prints developed in their own right with risk and adventure, drawn directly on to the plate and worked up through stages. Rembrandt's prints are not translations but images resolved within their making, with a high degree of improvisation. He understood the capacity for radically changing an image through burnishing and removing lines, for incorporating the engraved line as a value alongside the etched line. Since Rembrandt printed his own work he was also able to explore the possibilities of how the image could be transformed through wiping the plate, essentially bringing his painterly sensibility into print. This, along with his capacity as a draughtsman *par excellence*, enabled Rembrandt to produce a body of etchings that stand as a landmark in the history of printmaking. His approach is clearly evident in States III and IV of the *Three Crosses*, 1653, showing how dramatically the image could be transformed, leading the viewer to "believe that (they were) looking at impressions from two different plates".[6] "Light and shadow are now the principle actors: radiating, ricocheting streaks of animate shadow crisscross the scene, shattering solid forms into flickering fragments."[7]

GIOVANNI BATTISTA PIRANESI, *The Gothic Arch*, plate XIV, from the series *Carceri*, 1749.
Etching and engraving, 40 x 53 cm.

Furthermore, Rembrandt worked directly on to many of his plates from observation, his self-portraits, for example, are the immediate record of the act of looking, the plate and etching tool, substituting for the pencil on paper. These informal directly drawn prints capture that moment where the artist seeks a graphic equivalent to an observed moment in time.

Etching provided a perfect vehicle to explore light and darkness with its capacity to render rich deep blacks and Giovanni Battista Piranesi spectacularly used this quality in his etched series *Carceri* (*Prisons*). These were large-format prints, 40 x 53 cm published in 1745 and produced as folios. These fantastic scenes of imagined buildings are imbued with the romantic idea of the ruin, the building opened out and exposed to view with its crumbling masonry, high vaulted ceilings and mysterious staircases, leading the viewer through the dark, labyrinthine space. The plates are drawn with a directness and vigour, reminiscent of Rembrandt, but here, the physicality of etching is taken further, with the lines deeply bitten and dark shadows formed from the mesh of lines.

Alongside these innovators, many artists used etching and engraving as a means to publish their ideas and reach a wider public. The function of print has often been to adopt an alternative position to painting's official role within the establishment. It is largely through print that we can gather a sense of the hardships, suffering and indeed pleasures of the general population. In England, for example, Hogarth produced a great number of prints including important suites made after his paintings including, *A Harlot's Progress*, 1733, followed by *The Rake's Progress*, 1734, depicting moral tales of debauchery and generally serving as a critical condemnation of the period. The original paintings for *A Harlot's Progress* were destroyed in a fire so it is only through these prints that these images are now known, a reminder of the important function prints have as a means of preserving as well as distributing ideas.

In etching, tone had to be rendered through either cross-hatched lines or ink held on the surface. Mezzotint, developed in the seventeenth century, substituted line for tone. With mezzotint the whole plate is 'rocked' with hundreds of lines incised into the surface to create a plate with a roughed surface that will print an overall dense black. From this starting point of black, tones could then be created by burnishing and polishing areas of the plate to make lighter passages. The advantage of the process was in that it allowed a continuous tonal range from rich blacks through to white. This proved ideal as a means of reproduction, perfect for translating the soft tones of oil painting but was rarely used by artists themselves in a creative way. The mezzotints made by David Lucas after the paintings of John Constable are a good example of how the process was used to reproduce existing paintings and show the degree of skill required on behalf of the printer. Other examples are the dramatic mezzotints made after John Martin for the publication of *Paradise Lost*, published in 1826, or the numerous prints made after paintings by the Pre-Raphaelites. More recently, contemporary artists have been attracted to the process particularly for rendering work with a strong feeling of photographic realism as in the works of Mark Balakjian or Katsunori Hamanishi.

An alternative solution to the problem of making tone was aquatint. It was developed in Holland around the same time as mezzotint but was not really taken up by artists until the eighteenth century. While mezzotint imitated oil painting, aquatint was initially developed to render the tones of watercolour and wash drawings. But it was the Spanish artist, Francisco Goya who first used it for its own intrinsic qualities.

Goya was able to use aquatint with a freedom, urgency and economy that matched the fluency and impulse of his drawings. Aquatint required working from light through to dark, 'stopping out' the light areas first before immersing

top: FRANCISCO GOYA, *And it can't be helped* from *The Disasters of War*, 1810–1820 (published in 1863).
A collection of 80 plates drawn and etched, 14 x 17 cm.

bottom: FRANCISCO GOYA, *What more can one do?* from *The Disasters of War*, 1810–1820 (published in 1863).
A collection of 80 plates drawn and etched, 15.5 x 20.5 cm.

the plate in acid. Working progressively and through multiple immersions, a range of tones could be achieved, the lightest being those immersed for the least time while the darkest tones would have been immersed for substantially longer. In *Por que fue sensible*, 1797–1798, Goya creates a compelling image exclusively through aquatint. However, in most cases, he used aquatint in conjunction with etching, often registering a sky or landscape with a single sweep of tone with the line drawing bleeding through. In Goya, both line and tone are given equal freedom, instilling these haunting images with a sense of movement and spontaneity as in *What more can one do?*, from *The Disasters of War*, 1810–1820. The apparent speed of execution of these prints, which at first glance appears deceptively simple, adds to the urgency of their deeply humanistic message.

In the nineteenth century, Edgar Degas is particularly interesting from a contemporary viewpoint for the way he used etching and aquatint as an experimental field for developing compositions. His prints, which go through many states, seem part of an ongoing exploration, exploiting the capacity for etching to carry the memory of each stage through to the next. He also produced a substantial body of experimental monotypes, cleaning away the ink with cloths and working back with brushes and sticks to evoke images reminiscent of photographs. All reveal his thinking process and offer insights into how he refined his visual ideas through materiality. While rarely exhibited in his own time, Degas' prints, particularly the monotypes, are now highly regarded and exert a growing influence on a wide range of contemporary artists, from the figurative to the abstract, who respond to their experimental and painterly qualities.

This spirit of experimentation underpins the graphic work of Pablo Picasso, who, building upon the likes of Rembrandt, Goya and Degas, produced a vast body of prints, in etching, lithography and linocut, innovating in all these media and transforming the way in which printmaking was seen. "For Picasso, printmaking is an art in itself; it is never used simply as a way of reproducing another work."[8]

Intaglio provided Picasso with a medium that was perfect to capture his fluid and impulsive line. Every stage and development of Picasso's *œuvre* finds its counterpoint in etchings, from the early *Le Repas Frugal*, 1904, from his Blue Period, through his Cubist compositions to his later work. Between 1930 and 1937 he produced the series known as *The Vollard Suite* after the publisher Ambroise Vollard, consisting of 100 etchings which serve as a visual diary of his preoccupying themes and concerns. "A major theme of the Vollard Suite is the Sculptor's Studio, which is represented in 46 plates, almost half the series. Of these, an astonishing 40... were produced between 20 March and 5 May 1933."[9]

These prints see Picasso in complete control of the media, utilising the full range of possibilities, from the simplest line through to complex cross-hatching and the use of burnishing as a drawing tool. For Picasso, it is as if every change of mind or correction is a positive step from which to drive the image to completion. Areas of the plate, which have been burnished, are left as tone, serving to render the transparency of a curtain or the texture of skin. *Minotauromachie*, 1935, one of Picasso's greatest prints, serves to show how complex and intense an image he could construct within the format of etching. Evolved over many states, it prefigures *Guernica* and orchestrates Picasso's complex private iconography with the myth of the Minotaur, the crucifixion and the drama of the bullfight.

In contrast to the output and innovation of Picasso, the Italian artist Giorgio Morandi used simple line and cross-hatching to create his etchings. Working from a narrow range of subjects, primarily landscapes and flowers or, most notably, still lifes drawn from bottles and other household items, which he would then reconfigure over and over again to form new compositions. He used the convention of cross-hatching and developed it into a subtle language where landscapes or still lifes are delicately held within a web of lines. Seen as an artists' artist, these prints in their restraint, concentrated focus and exploration of a formal visual language make them key references for a number of contemporary artists from Sean Scully through to Christopher Le Brun. They represent perfect control in their creation, with Morandi testing the strength of the acid prior to etching the actual plate, to ensure that the fine cross-hatched lines retained their precision and clarity.

In Paris in the late 1920s, Stanley William Hayter, a British artist, was very influential in bringing an experimental painterly approach to intaglio, not only through the example of his own work, but also through his studio, Atelier 17. This reflected the innovative approaches to painting, pioneered by the Surrealists, but Hayter was able to bring into print those qualities of chance, improvisation and freedom, particularly in his approach to colour. He developed a process of

GIORGIO MORANDI, *Still Life (Natura Morta)*, 1929.
Etching, 15 x 20.5 cm. Image courtesy Estorick Collection. © DACS 2009.

'viscosity printing' through which a multiple coloured image could be pulled from a single plate by etching it at differing depths and using inks of different consistency or viscosity. Through this process he was able to produce free flowing abstract prints, rich in colour. He was influential as a teacher and through his studio introduced many of the avant-garde artists of the day, including Joan Miró, Jean Arp and Yves Tanguy, to the potential of printmaking. When he moved to New York in 1940, his studio once again became a centre, attracting a new generation of American artists including Willem de Kooning, Jackson Pollock and David Smith.

Meanwhile, in the UK, Anthony Gross and the Portuguese artist Bartolomeu dos Santos, developed major bodies of work, one using etching and engraving, the other aquatint, raising the profile of printmaking and through their teaching at the Slade School of Art, creating a legacy that continues today. Gross built on Hayter's free use of line bringing vibrancy through engraving to his landscapes and observations of life. His works are full of light and air and the line takes on an independent spirit as if the line itself was dancing, a quality he was also to develop through experiments with animation. By contrast, dos Santos' brooding aquatints of ghostly bishops and dark labyrinths evoke Goya and the Surrealist filmmaker, Luis Buñuel. Dos Santos took the principles of etching further through large-scale public commissions where he etched and inked up limestone to form vast murals for public buildings.

While for many Pop artists screenprint was the ideal medium, with its capacity to print bold flat colours and photographic images, David Hockney looked back to etching, lithography and to drawing. In the most famous of his early prints, *A Rake's Progress*, 1961–1963 a series which reinterprets the engravings of Hogarth, the prints have an almost casual air, a range of pictorial languages and styles are jarringly brought together. The titles are stamped into each image as a conscious formal device, a reminder to the viewer of their flatness. Some of Hockney's finest work lies within printmaking, an ideal vehicle for his formidable skill as a draughtsman, from the subtle aquatints of Grimm's Fairy Tales, the elegant line etchings of his *Illustrations for Fourteen Poems from CP Cavafy* through to the complex, colourful images for *The Blue Guitar*. In America, the Pop artist Jim Dine was also able to use etching in a contemporary way, focusing on individual objects such as tools or brushes, which through his hand, become individualised and charged with personality. His etching *Braid*, 1973, is a beautiful example of his ability to make a memorable image from an isolated object. Dine's work has resonance with the prints of Wenceslaus Hollar, the seventeenth century Czech artist whose intense still life images featured amongst other things, fur ruffs and shells, inducing an erotic presence within these inanimate scenes.

The Spanish artist Antoni Tàpies has been a prolific and inventive printmaker, creating works which reflect his passion for surfaces and the calligraphic gestural mark. He has frequently combined processes, used intaglio alongside other mediums

ANTHONY GROSS, *Arab Horse Bath*, 1954.
Etching, 23.5 x 38.5 cm, signed with the alternate title *Chez les Druses* and numbered 23/50. Image courtesy The Redfern Gallery. © The Estate of Anthony Gross RA and The Redfern Gallery, London.

including carborundum, as a means of painting directly on to the plate, and through this recording the gesture as a physical and embossed mark. His interest in creating resonate surfaces in his paintings have also resulted in prints which use impressions of clothing, such as vests and socks, as part of the printing process, with these items inked and embossed into the paper.

Etching has retained its attraction to artists into the present. Whilst it must be said that, too often, it is the precious qualities the process affords, the embossed plate mark, complete with decal and printer's stamp, which can turn an indifferent sketch into a desirable and marketable commodity, numerous artists have shown how open the process is to contemporary practice. Lucian Freud has produced a large number of etchings, focusing on building up a form through line, where the prints operate inbetween his drawing and paintings. The prints, whilst retaining their structured observation of the figure in space, extend the possibilities of drawing using a myriad of lines.

The Portuguese artist Paula Rego, in her series *The Nursery Rhymes*, references the language of Goya through line and aquatint, to produce images of childhood and remembered events. These prints, within the mainstream canon of printmaking and on a scale of children's illustrations, have been widely exhibited throughout the world since they were first published in 1989, serving to connect her to an audience beyond that which is possible simply through her paintings and pastels. Her suites of subsequent prints have responded to a variety of texts including *Peter Pan* and *Jane Eyre*, in each case taking an oblique view on a familiar text, filtered through her own stories and experience. In 1999, she used etching as a means to engage in the recent debate on abortion in Portugal, by producing a series of prints based on her large pastels to graphically portray the suffering and isolation of those forced to seek unlicensed terminations.

William Kentridge has also used print to evoke social change. A South African artist, his work soundly confronted apartheid using etching to satirise the political system and highlight the moral consequences of the regime. The relationship between his prints and his hand-drawn animated films is rich and interconnected, with each informing the other.

The sculptor Louise Bourgeois has produced a startling body of work through print, many of which have been simple drypoints, or in some cases using a sewn line as the graphic device, referring back to her family history of tapestry restorers. Like Rego, it is drawing in all its guises that distinguish her prints, from the scribbled note, the passing thought through to more complex works. The counterpoint between the prints and the sculptures offers telling insights into the origins of her art, and, while her sculptures are increasingly public works, the prints are reminders of a private, quite secretive imaginative source. Kiki Smith's prints also have a direct correlation to her sculpture, in her case, paper being the key element in both. In a print such as *Peacock*, 1997, the image of the bird is formed across ten sheets of delicate Japanese paper, giving it an object-like presence with the same fragility as her sculptural works, the sections of paper suggesting the unfolding display of the bird's plumage.

LITHOGRAPHY

Lithography was first developed as a commercial process to print sheet music in 1798 by Alois Senefelder, based on the simple principle that ink and water repelled one another. The artist, by drawing with greasy materials, inks or crayons, on to a prepared limestone or later metal plate, was able to have their design directly translated into ink on paper. Lithography had a number of advantages; it was fast, it was able to print colour in a precise way (in etching the colour can be altered depending on the metal used), registration was relatively simple, the limestone blocks available were large in comparison to that which was possible through etching, and they were reusable. With the later development of offset printing, the artist was also able to work without the problem of the image being reversed. Initially the process was used as a drawing medium. Its capacity to be printed alongside text made it attractive for use in publications. In France, Honoré Daumier produced lithographs on an almost daily basis for various newspapers and journals, most importantly for *Le Charivari*, making almost 4,000 lithographs during his lifetime.

Artists, such as Eugène Delacroix, responded to lithography's capacity to produce soft tones and through this were able to bring their drawings to a wider audience of collectors. Goya's series *The Bulls of Bordeaux*, 1825, showed how he was able to build upon his use of aquatint and utilise the greater freedom inherent in crayon drawing through lithography. The use of this new medium by artists gathered pace in the late nineteenth century with superb prints by Henri Fantin-Latour and Odilon Redon, both of whom exploited the range of tones possible in this new medium. Fantin-Latour used it to subtly render skin tones while Redon used the black as a depth of space from which to conjure his dark imagination.

Towards the end of the nineteenth century, particularly in Paris, colour lithography began to be used by artists to make multicolour images. While many of the advantages of lithography were in commercial terms, for the artist the process allowed for the brush mark to be directly translated into print in a way that had not been possible before. While relief, etching and engraving were processes ideally suited to drawing, lithography brought the painter's concerns, his tools and materials, into the print studio. However, it was the interest in Japanese woodblock prints that can be seen to provide the catalyst for showing how artists could use this new process to develop colour images. The Japanese prints with their economical use of colour and bold designs provided a master class for artists working with lithography, but with the added bonus that the drawing of the plate could rest in the hand of the artist, rather than relying on the craftsman to cut the blocks.

Colour printing in lithography is a very subtle art, the inks behaving more like watercolour in their transparency, allowing the possibility for overlays and optical mixes. Furthermore, through diluting the ink and using washes, each colour could be gradated from pale through to full strength. The skilled lithographer was able to create the impression of numerous colours while actually only printing a few, a great commercial advantage, since, as already mentioned with Japanese woodblocks, each extra printing of colour carried an extra cost.

Henri de Toulouse-Lautrec's posters for the Paris music halls used all of lithography's attributes. Printed as commercial posters, lithography gave the artist the option of working directly and quickly on a relatively large scale. Colour printing was fast and therefore images could be out on to the street relatively quickly in order to advertise a particular performance or event.

Lautrec seized on lithography as a process most suited to his bold use of design, clearly inspired by Japanese woodcut prints. His inventiveness and experimentation through the media, printing large areas of flat colour alongside delicate crayon drawing extended lithography's graphic potential for artists. Working with gum stencils and splattering ink as well as crayons, these prints take on a physicality and sense of the surface being an arena for action, a quality that would be taken further by the American artists in the 1960s and 70s. Pierre Bonnard and Édouard Vuillard also found this medium ideally suited to their refined sense of colour. They were able to give the impression of a rich palette with relatively few printings, using overlay to create additional colours (the optical mix of one colour on top of the next) and exploiting the colour value of the paper itself. Whilst modest in size, their prints retain a fresh and informal quality and have been highly influential to subsequent generations of printmakers.

HENRI FANTIN-LATOUR, *The Bouquet of Roses*, 1879.
Chalk lithograph, 41.5 x 35.5 cm.

ODILON REDON, *The Eye Like a Strange Balloon Mounts Toward Infinity*, 1882.
Lithograph, 26 x 19.5 cm.

The use of lithography as a means of producing posters was not confined to the *joie de vivre* in Paris. It became the media through which revolutions were orchestrated with lithographic posters serving revolutionary ideals in Russia, Cuba and China. Commercially, lithography was used to advertise everything from soap to the cinema, as well as a tool for governments in calling young men to war. In Britain, many artists, including John Piper, Ben Nicholson and Graham Sutherland, were involved in designing posters for amongst others, the General Post Office (GPO), London Underground, Shell-Mex and British Petroleum (BP) and for Ealing Studios. There was considerable freedom in these projects, their function being to inform and celebrate rather than sell, offering the artist considerable latitude. A further example of the social function of print can be seen in the School's Prints project in the 1940s where many of the leading artists of the time were commissioned to make a lithograph in a large edition to be distributed to schools to provide, what was for many, their first introduction to modern art. Artists included Julian Trevelyan, Feliks Topolski, LS Lowry, Georges Braque, Henri Matisse and Pablo Picasso.

Braque, Matisse and Picasso all produced substantial and important bodies of work through lithography and by considering their different approaches, insights can be drawn about their very different personalities. Braque's major printworks through this medium enable his compositions to have a completeness that puts them on a par with his paintings. The colour is sonorous and perfectly orchestrated. Nowhere is this more apparent than in *Théière et Citrons*, 1949, where Braque's ability to transcend the modest still life subject matter, to make an image of monumental stability through a controlled orchestration of colour, is unparalleled. Picasso and Matisse in contrast used the richness of black and white rather than colour. Matisse focused on the use of crayon drawing to produce sensuous images of his models where the touch of crayon on the surface of the stone is almost palpable. Matisse extends his drawing through lithography, taking them to a greater degree of resolution. Picasso's images are predominantly painted with tusche (a greasy drawing ink), the medium responding to the nuance of his brushwork and subject to physical re-working in which the image would be radically transformed, stage by stage, as if each was a new start. Not content with pulling a single edition from the stone, Picasso frequently reworked the image editioning the same print at various stages. Through this Picasso has left a visual record of the dramatic changes and transformations that an image might be subjected to, recorded through the various editions pulled. In both Picasso's etchings and lithographs there is a wonderful feeling of him only wishing to go forward, revisions registering as positive elements, their trace only adding to the urgency of their conception.

In post-revolutionary Mexico, printmaking, and in particular lithography, attracted artists such as Diego Rivera, David Alfaro Siqueros and José Clemente Orozco to produce prints and posters which would be available to the general public and address a wide audience. Their strong graphic style, coupled with dynamic compositions made printmaking an ideal vehicle for the depiction of their revolutionary ideals and everyday life. Posters celebrated the political struggle, called workers to become unionised and voiced opposition to fascism while in

HENRI DE TOULOUSE-LAUTREC, *The Clowness at the Moulin Rouge*, 1897.
Lithograph, 41 x 32 cm.

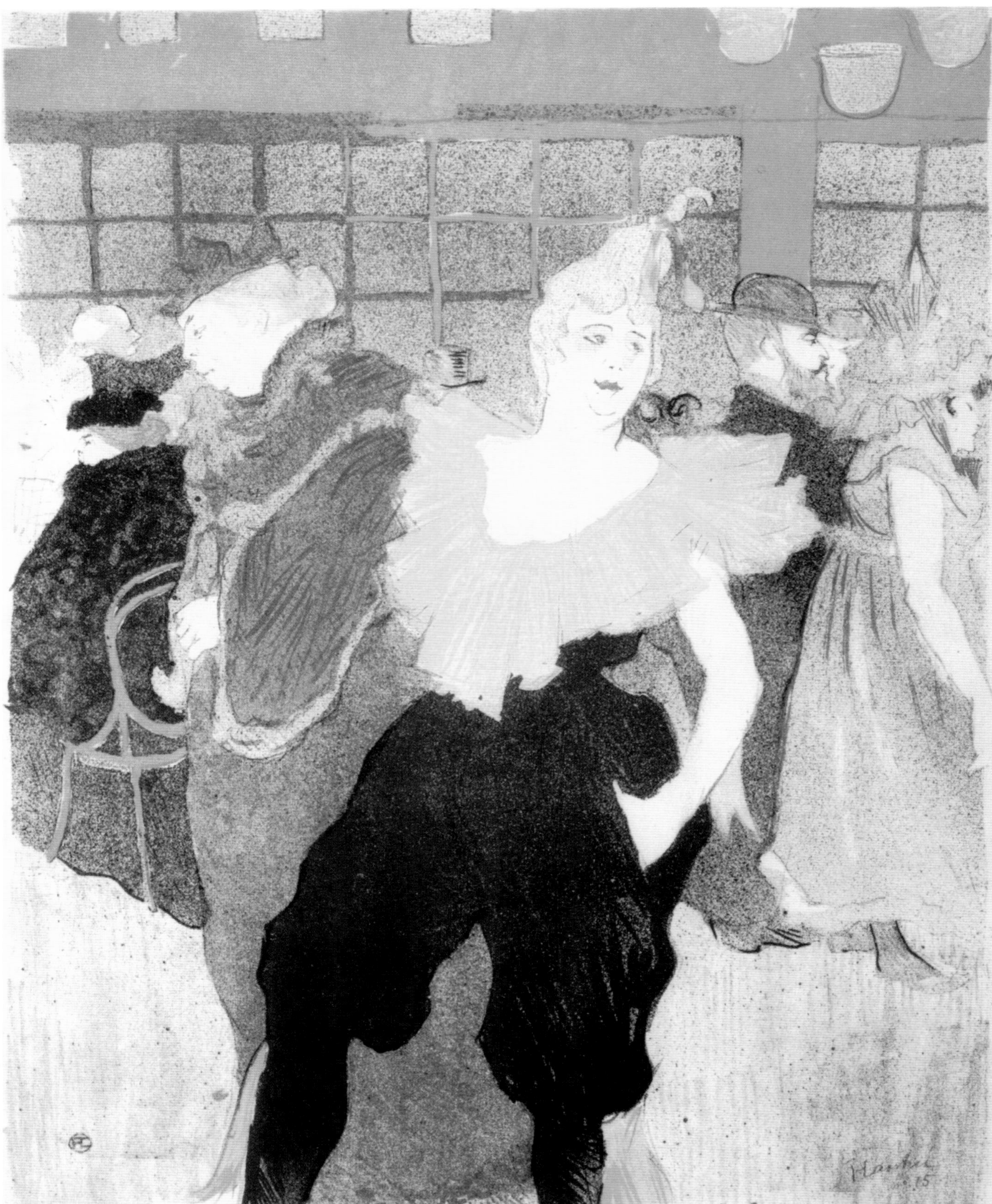

ÉDOUARD VUILLARD, *La Pâtisserie* from *Paysages et Intérieurs*, 1899.
One of 12 lithographs printed in seven colours on China paper, 35.5 x 27 cm.

ALBERTO GIACOMETTI, *Interieur de café*, 1959–1964.
Planche 20 de *Paris sans fins*, lithographie sur velin d'Arches, 42 x 32 cm. Coll. Fondation Giacometti, Paris (inv. 1994-0830). © Fondation Giacometti, Paris, 2009, © ADAGP/FAAG, Paris and DACS, London 2009.

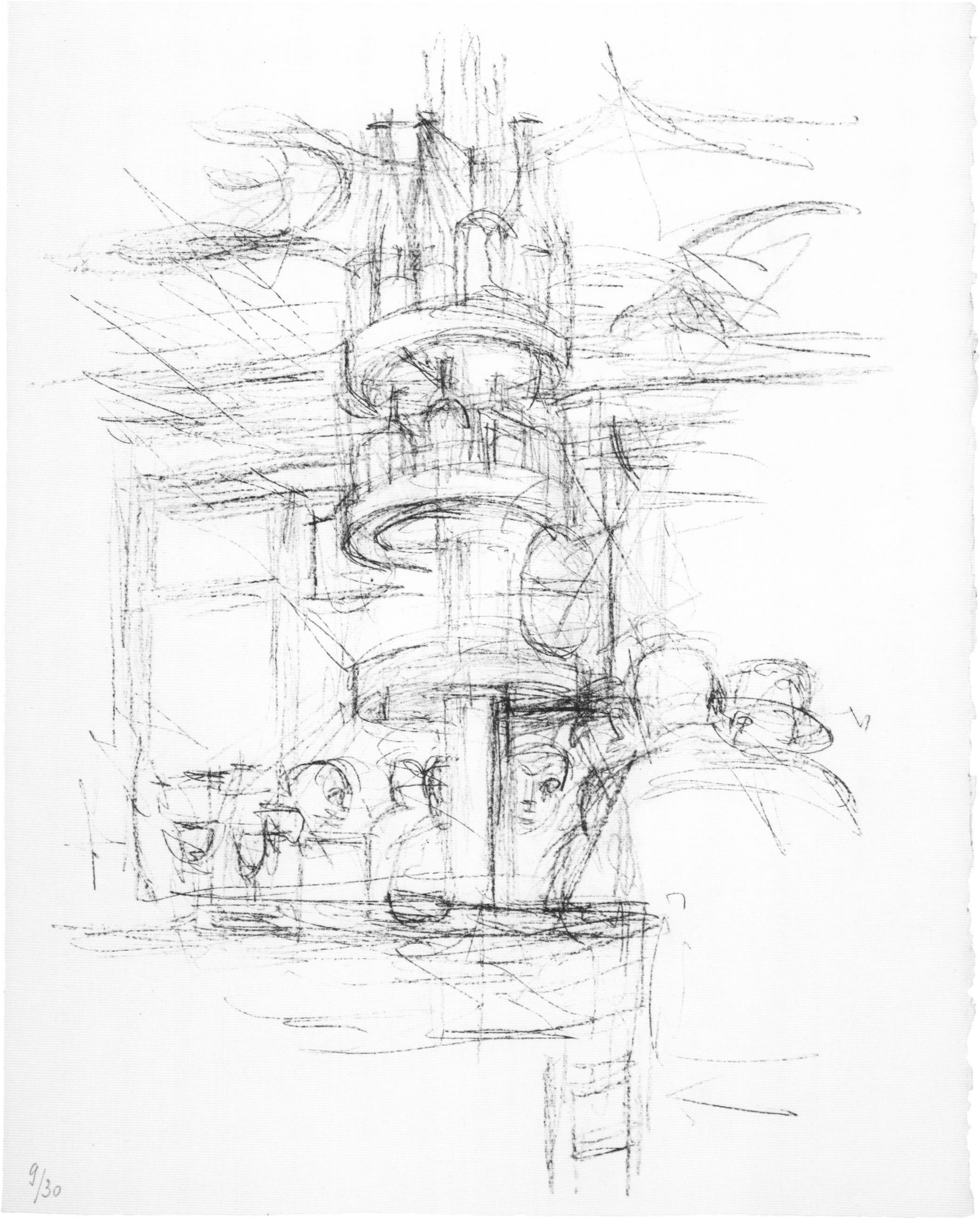

ROBERT RAUSCHENBERG, *Booster*, from the series *Booster and 7 Studies*, 1967.
Lithograph and sceenprint, 183.5 x 90.5 cm. Digital image: The Museum of Modern Art, New York/Scala, Florence. © Estate of Robert Rauschenberg. DACS, London/VAGA, New York 2009.

individual prints they drew upon the mural tradition and reflected the desire to form a modern Mexican art. Printmaking, unlike painting, was perceived to represent the people, reflecting the tradition of popular art and drawing inspiration from amongst others, José Guadalupe Posada. "In post-revolutionary Mexico, the rhetoric about the new freedom and rights of the Mexican people was accompanied by the idea of an art of and for the people."[10]

It was not only through lithography, but also through woodcut and linoleum prints, that these Mexican artists found a means to both forward their political and social views whilst also developing a strong unique tradition in which printmaking was positioned as the medium of choice.

Between 1957 and 1962, towards the end of his life, the Swiss born artist, Alberto Giacometti produced a series of 150 lithographs, which formed the book, *Paris sans fin*, 1969. These prints, which record the artist's memories of Paris, are directly drawn in crayon, and are reliant on his strength both as a draughtsman and of the process being sensitive to the recording of the lightest touch. Whilst in these prints the artist employs the simplest approach to lithography, as a series they stand as one of the great monuments of modern art.

In America, there was already a growing tradition of lithography in the early half of the twentieth century, George Bellows using it to great effect to develop his illustrations—most famously in his series of boxing prints. This is a further reminder of the way print can engage with an audience not necessarily educated in art, through popular subject matter and the relatively cheap multiple image.

Lithography underwent a transformation in the early 1960s, led by the establishment of a number of workshops including Pratt Graphics Center, Tamarind Lithography Workshop and Universal Limited Art Editions, which together acted as advocates for the medium and encouraged the emerging generation of artists to experiment with print. The medium of lithography was readily in tune with the tenets of Abstract Expressionism, with its emphasis on the gesture and brush mark and in the renewed interest in Eastern calligraphy. The ambition and invention shown by the studios reflected an optimism about the modern world and an excitement for technical innovation. It also coincided with New York's position as the centre for contemporary art, and a growing prosperous middle class with a desire to be connected with the future rather than the past.

While in Europe, paper was generally seen as a neutral element, the substrate to receive the image, in the United States, increasingly, paper became an embedded part of the print as a whole, the print seen as a complete object rather than merely an image on paper. Studios worked with artists in a spirit of innovation and risk, keen to extend and challenge preconceptions of what might constitute a print. This is clearly demonstrated in Robert Rauschenberg's *Booster*, 1967, which combined lithography with screenprint—it measures over two metres in height and brought together imagery which included a full length x-ray of the artist in his boots! Rauschenberg's contribution is immense in extending the boundaries of printmaking, for example, in his 1974 series *Hoarfrost*, newspaper images were printed on to overlaid silk chiffon and incorporated in collaged paper bags.

Print also has a function in revealing an artist's working method, through producing works in series or portfolios. Whilst a series of paintings would rarely be kept together, the cost of purchasing a suite of paintings often being prohibitive, through the folio, the artist's intention could both be preserved and widely distributed. In Jasper Johns' *Color Numerals Series*, 1968, the individual prints not only function in their own right, but when seen together, become a visual essay articulating the artist's thinking process. It is also useful to note in this series, the inventive use of the rainbow roll, blending the colour on the roller itself before inking up the plate.

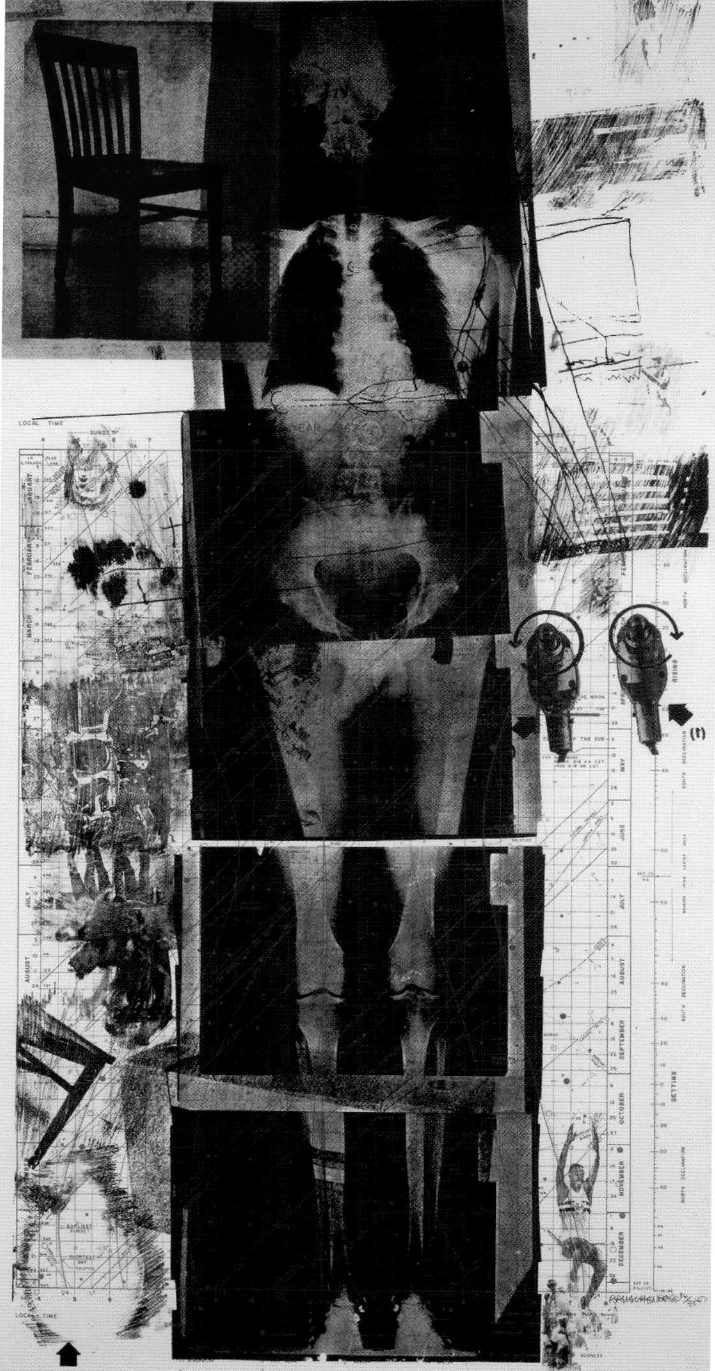

PATRICK CAULFIELD, *Garden with Pines*, 1975.
Screenprint, paper and image 77.5 x 102.5 cm, edition of 70. Published by Waddington Graphics, London. Courtesy the Estate of Patrick Caulfield and Alan Cristea Gallery, London.

SCREENPRINT

Screenprinting was another commercial process that has been taken up by artists to produce multiple images of their work. While it was originated centuries before, it was adapted as a commercial process in the 1950s. Screenprinting was fast and perfect for printing large areas of flat colour as well as half-tone photographic images. These two qualities made it the process of choice in the 1960s for a number of artists working within the Pop movement. The process perfectly reflected the concerns of Pop and its engagement with advertising, text and commercial processes. Screenprint was ideal for Roy Lichtenstein whose style was based on the Ben-Day Dot system as used in comics, to develop images which were reliant on sharp outlines and flat colour. Lichtenstein went on to produce a major body of work through print, using lithography and woodcut as well as screenprint. For the British artist, Patrick Caulfield, screenprint was his only print media, providing the means to produce images using large flat areas of saturated colour, held in place by his trademark black line, an example of how the detachment of the process of screenprint could be used to create works of intense visual poetry.

Eduardo Paolozzi, working with the printer Chris Prater, took the process of screenprinting to new heights in terms of complexity and registration, producing a number of works such as in *Calcium Night Light*, 1974–1976, a series of prints for Charles Ives' *Four German Songs*. These works form an almost mosaic-like surface, printed with a breathtaking number of layers. While this was ambitious in 1974, in 2004 the artist Chuck Close, working with Pace Editions, produced *JAMES*, a screenprint made with 178 colours.

In the UK, Richard Hamilton made a series of iconic works through screenprint which seem to epitomise the swinging 60s and the relationship between art and fashion. He used a photograph of Mick Jagger and the art dealer, Robert Fraser handcuffed on their way to trial for possession of drugs for a series of prints *Swingeing London 67*, 1967–1968, while in *My Marilyn*, 1965, a sheet of

PATRICK CAULFIELD, *Les Demoiselles d'Avignon vues de Derrière*, 1999.
Screenprint on Somerset paper, paper 132 x 111.5 cm / image 106 x 92 cm, edition of 65. Printed at Advanced Graphics, London. Published by Alan Cristea Gallery, London. Courtesy the Estate of Patrick Caulfield and Alan Cristea Gallery, London.

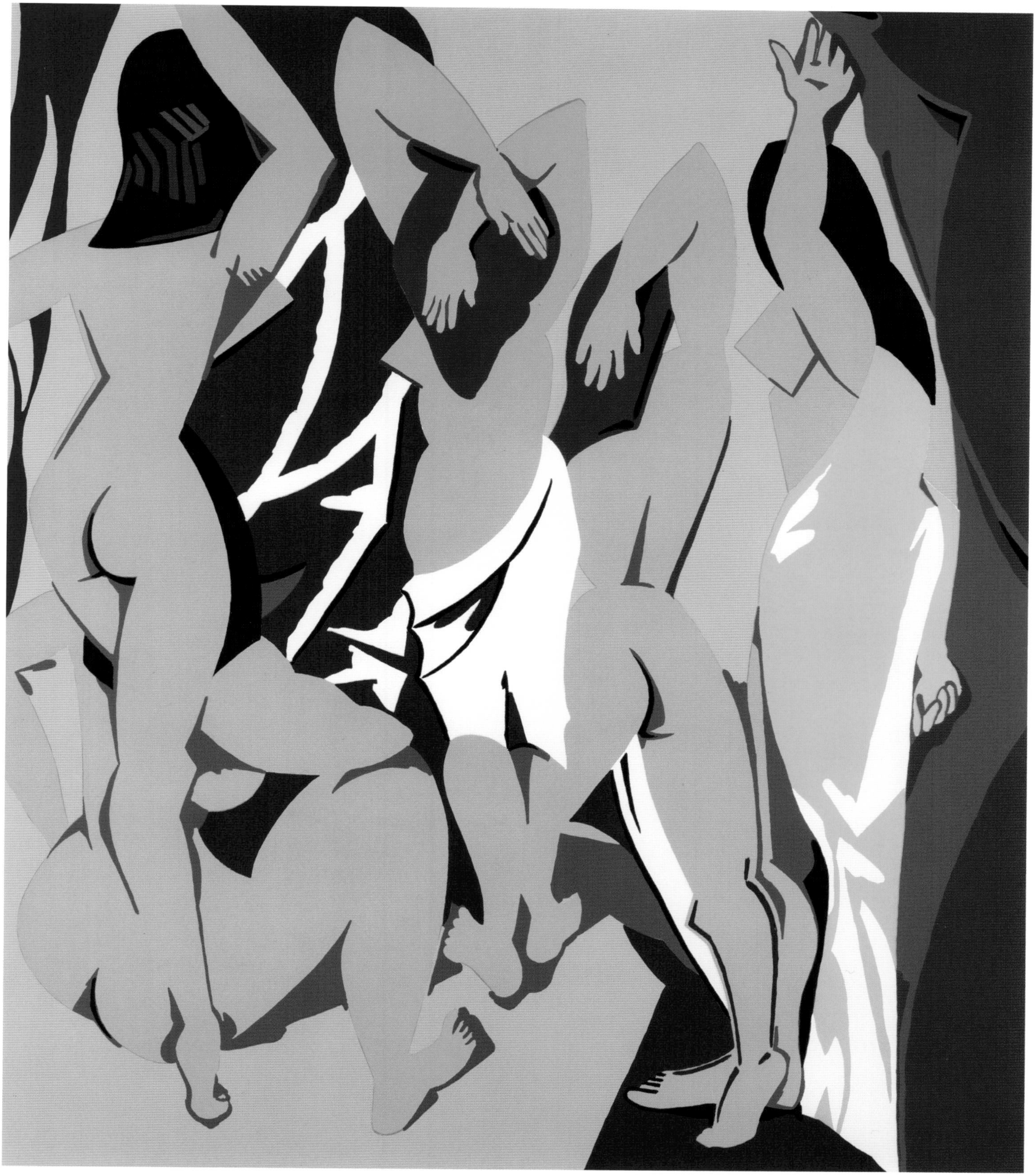

PATRICK CAULFIELD, *She'll have forgotten her scarf* from *Some Poems of Jules Laforgue Edition C*, 1973.

A series of 22 screenprints bound into a book illustrating 12 poems and published in three varying editions A, B & C, paper 61 x 56 cm / image 40.5 x 35.5 cm, edition of 100. Proofed by Advanced Graphics, London, and editioned by Frank Kicherer, Stuttgart. Books, sleeves, slipcases, and portfolios bound in full leather by Rudolph Rieser, Cologne. Published by Petersburg Press in association with Waddington Galleries, London. Courtesy the Estate of Patrick Caulfield and Alan Cristea Gallery, London.

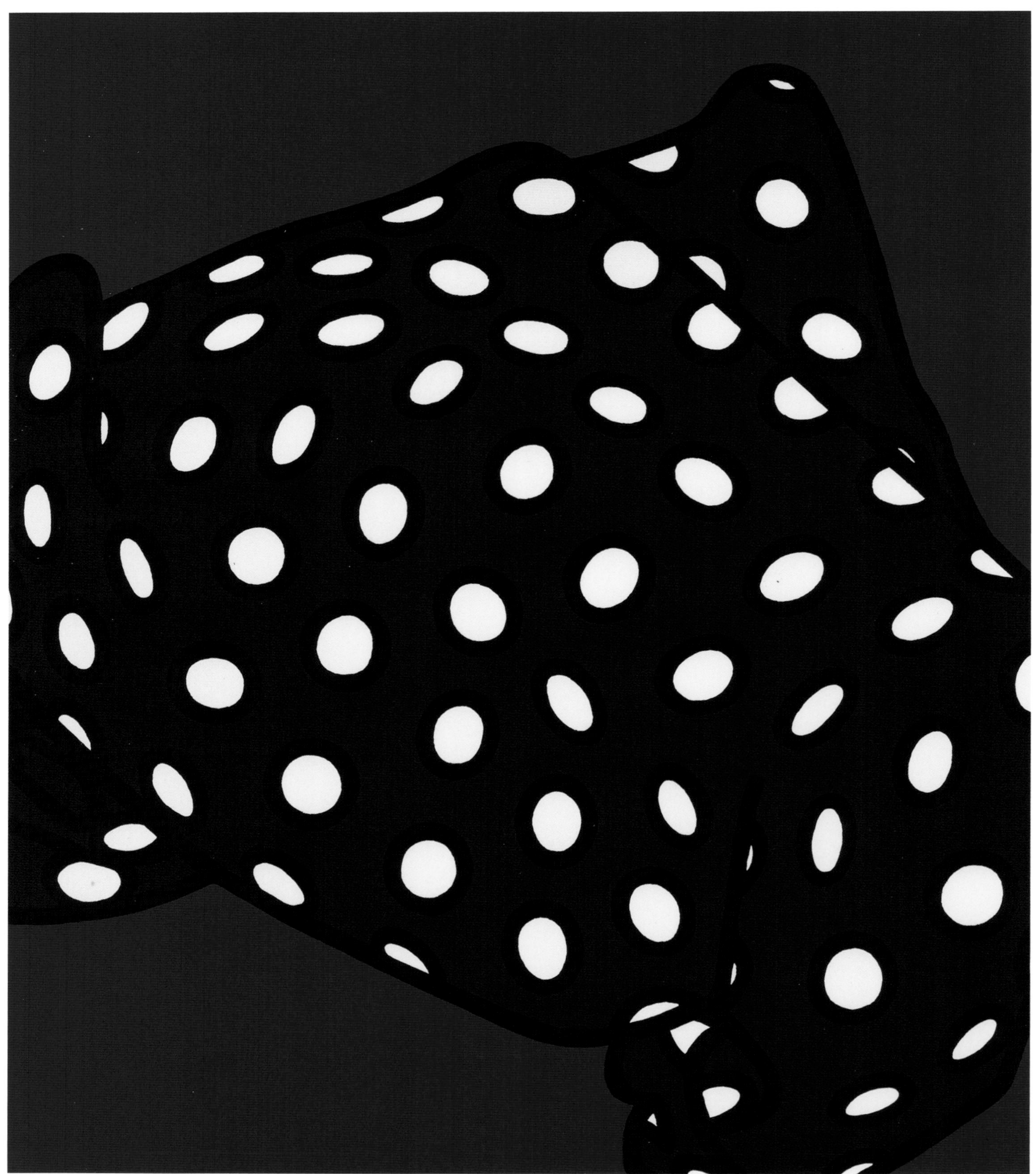

PATRICK CAULFIELD, *Oh Helen, I roam my room*, from *Some Poems of Jules Laforgue Edition C*, 1973.
A series of 22 screenprints bound into a book illustrating 12 poems and published in three varying editions A, B & C, paper 61 x 56 cm / image 40.5 x 35.5 cm, edition of 100. Proofed by Advanced Graphics, London, and editioned by Frank Kicherer, Stuttgart. Books, sleeves, slipcases, and portfolios bound in full leather by Rudolph Rieser, Cologne. Published by Petersburg Press in association with Waddington Galleries, London. Courtesy the Estate of Patrick Caulfield and Alan Cristea Gallery, London.

RICHARD HAMILTON, *My Marilyn (a)*, 1965.
Screenprint from 11 stencils on cartridge paper, paper 69 x 102 / image 54.5 x 64 cm (dimensions vary), edition of 17 varied impressions. Printed by the artist at University of Newcastle-upon-Tyne. Image courtesy Alan Cristea Gallery, London. © Richard Hamilton, all rights reserved, DACS 2009.

ANDY WARHOL, *Brillo Boxes*, 1964.
Synthetic polymer paint and silkscreen on wood, 43.5 x 43 x 36.5 cm. Digital image: The Museum of Modern Art, New York/Scala, Florence. © The Andy Warhol Foundation for the Visual Arts / Artists Rights Society (ARS), New York / DACS, London 2009.

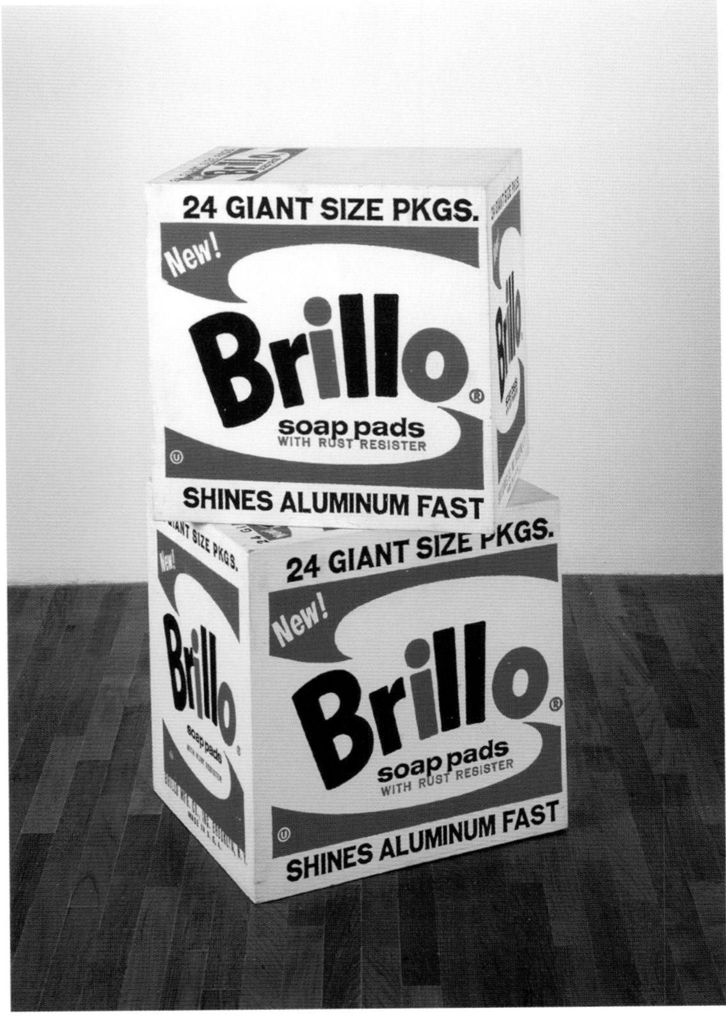

photographs for approval by Marilyn Monroe becomes the starting point for a print exploring the nature of photography. Throughout his career Hamilton has used print with an almost unrivalled intelligence, fitting subject matter to the medium in a continuous questioning of language and the role of the multiple image. His work has ranged from hand-drawn images through to photographic collages, but all celebrate the idea of the mechanically produced image.

However, it was Andy Warhol who took screenprint as his own, and used the squeegee as a substitute for the brush, the detachment inherent in the process suiting his philosophy of wanting to work like a machine and transforming his studio into a factory.

While other artists endeavoured to control the process and create exact registration, Warhol's work has an apparent 'throwaway' informality, registration appearing almost casual. His paintings were made through the same screenprinting process, often recording the gradual filling in of the stencil as if it was a marker of time passing. With Warhol there is a short step from subject matter, either his own photographs or appropriated imagery, through to final print. His print work is an inventory of late twentieth century imagery, from celebrities, Marilyn Monroe, to Mao, from Campbell soup cans to dollar signs, and from old masters to the electric chair. Warhol used screenprint not only to make his prints and paintings, but also for the wallpaper for his exhibitions; *Cow Wallpaper* exhibited at the Leo Castelli Gallery in 1966 and in the printed surfaces of his *Brillo Box* sculptures, 1964.

Fine art and commercial printing have always been closely connected with many artists choosing to work within the commercial field of printmaking rather than the fine art studio. Marcel Duchamp, keen to remove himself from the physical act of production, used commercial printers to produce *La Boîte-en-Valise*, 1935–1941, in which he made miniature reproductions of his paintings and 'readymades'. Duchamp's use of print to conserve and distribute his ideas was also matched by a delight in the qualities of each reproduction. Ed Ruscha in his hugely influential books, such as *Twenty-six Gasoline Stations*, 1962, and *Various Small Fires*, 1964, used commercial black and white photolithography without any artifice. These books, published in large editions and distributed widely provide an alternative to the tradition of the *livres d'artiste* and fine art publishing with its emphasis on quality materials and high-end production.

Commercial printing, in the form of a postcard of Piccadilly Circus, provided the German artist Dieter Roth, with the subject matter for *6 Piccadillies*, 1970. In this series, printed in a combination of lithography and screenprint, he subjects the image to erasure, overprinting and obliteration. Inspired by Dada, Roth's approach to printmaking verged on the anarchistic, often incorporating actual bananas or chocolate into the image, which would in due course rot and degrade, the surface of the print functioning as a sort of petri dish to grow mould.

THE DIGITAL PRINT

The digital print originated in the 1960s when a few artists began to see how this new technology could be used as a graphic tool. Computers, however, were rare, often located within research institutions and were very slow. In addition, before commercially available software, an artist needed to either know how to program or work with a programmer in order to translate their ideas into a visual form. Output was also limited to often quite crude printouts on thin paper stock, or through flatbed ink plotters. Artists were generally restricted to black lines or else a very limited schematic colour range. These limitations, however, were also an attraction to a number of artists working with systems and code. The prints, rather than in the past being the result of a visual engagement with a matrix, were the manifestation of a series of commands. This is evidenced in the work of Herbert W Franke, one of the pioneers of digital printmaking whose prints explore a wide range of imagery from the geometric abstraction through to investigations based on photographs. Heike M Piehler, in the catalogue *Ex Machina* points to the experimental nature of his approach:

> It is not his intention to show the perfected work of art in isolation, for its own sake—on the contrary, it is to be seen as an example of what is fundamentally possible. As a consequence, his exhibits are always representative of artistic works that could be created just as easily by other artists who follow him, rather than Franke personally.[11]

Harold Cohen, a painter with an established reputation, became aware of the possibilities of the new technology following a period as visiting Professor at the University of California at San Diego in 1986. Later, while at Stanford University's Artificial Intelligence Lab, he developed AARON, an automatic drawing programme which explored the potential of artificial intelligence, and over a period of more than two decades, has produced thousands of drawings.[12]

The early digital artists were more like scientists, often working within research establishments or industries, borrowing time on expensive equipment. It is difficult to say how many of these artists would view their work within the tradition of printmaking, as it often seemed to occupy a territory where the emphasis was more on the nature of experimentation and the work, a consequence of pushing at the boundaries of technology. However, as the technology improved and became more widespread with the advent of the home computer and graphic software programmes, the potential for artists to engage with digital processes rapidly accelerated. Printmakers, used to the process of translation and mediation were well placed to take advantage of these new opportunities. The colour inkjet printer placed the artist in a totally new relationship to production. The artist could now draw, proof, publish and distribute in a way and with a speed impossible to have conceived of a generation before. The computer has essentially made everyone a potential printmaker in the same way that the instant camera empowered the general public as photographers.

The most noticeable development for printmakers has been in the availability of large-format colour inkjet printers. There were two immediate problems however to be resolved; first, the lightfast quality of the inks and, secondly, the limited range of papers. Originally, the inks were dye-based and very fugitive, with inkjet prints fading during the course of an exhibition. Obviously, this presented a big problem in selling the prints and, unfortunately, this suspicion lingered long after the issue was resolved with the introduction of pigment-based inks. The printers gradually became more robust and able to print on to an increasingly wide range of substrates, from plastics and cloth through to coated fine art papers. Furthermore, the printers became cheaper, the profit for the manufacturers moving from hardware to consumables, and their range increased, from desk top through to wide format on an industrial scale.

Richard Hamilton, whose lifelong engagement with technology through printmaking is well documented, was one of the first artists to really take advantage of the new landscape. In his print, *The Marriage*, 1998, he takes a discarded wedding photograph and proceeds to restore it, lovingly bringing it back to a sense of its original brilliance. It is perhaps ironic that while the debate was raging about the longevity of digital prints, Hamilton uses it to restore a previously faded technology. The Turner Prize winner, Grenville Davey, turned his eye, literally, to the building block of this new form of image-making, the pixel. In his portfolio of prints, *Eye*, 1993, he examines the tension between the image and how it is constituted, with the image, as it is enlarged, revealing its pixel structure. Paradoxically, the prints were made as screenprints and not inkjets.

Within digital printmaking, studios have become established and master printers acknowledged as with previous technologies. The boundaries between printmaking and photography have become blurred; once two distinct processes, they are now defined by histories and intention rather than the nature of the studio or darkroom, each accessing the same equipment and materials.

In printmaking, digital technology has brought two profound differences in the economics of production. First, that with digital prints an edition could be printed on demand, the unit cost of printing each print being the same. This is a dramatic change from more traditional printmaking where the artist was committed to printing a whole edition in one go. And secondly, while previously the dimensions of a print were fixed, a print from a digital file could vary according to need and be offered in any range of sizes, giving the buyer the option to have the print made to fit the location.

PRINTMAKING AN EXPANDED PRACTICE

Printmaking in the contemporary scene, is a multifaceted art, with processes overlapping, new processes coming into being and old technologies being revisited. While printmaking seems to be ever present, certain periods, generally fuelled by a rising middle class, have produced print booms, most notably in the 1960s and 1970s. While the scope of this text is very much focused on fine art prints, it is worth noting the explosion of interest in all forms of graphic expression during this period. Posters, particularly featuring rock bands, became an essential element in any student's bedroom. There was a proliferation of independent magazines, often with clear graphic identities such as in the notorious *Oz* magazine, while the LP record cover increasingly became a site for artists attention, the most memorable being Peter Blake's cover for The Beatles' *Sgt. Pepper's Lonely Hearts Club Band*, 1967, and, for the same group, Richard Hamilton's cool minimal typographic design for their *White Album*, 1968. Against this backdrop, there were opportunities to experiment and question what a print might be.

A number of print biennials particularly across Europe were initiated, including in Ljubljana, Kraków, and Bradford, which not only serve as a reminder of the importance of graphic media in Europe but also enable an exchange of ideas through the mobility of print. These biennials provided an important exchange between artists who made their own prints under often quite modest circumstances, and those artists working with a studio supported by technicians and underwritten by publishers.

Increasingly artists are keen to combine media and push the boundaries of printmaking. No one personifies this tendency more than Kenneth E Tyler. In the late 1960s Tyler established Gemini G.E.L and then in 1974, Tyler Graphics. He set new standards for ambition, scale and inventiveness in printmaking. Prints under Tyler's direction, freely combined a range of processes in their making, celebrating the notion of the hybrid print. His collaboration with Frank Stella took print into three dimensions with work of staggering complexity and engineering. Whist in works like *Time Dust*, 1992, by James Rosenquist, measuring over ten metres, the print took on the quality of mural painting. He also embraced papermaking as an element in the production of work, and in a series of inventive projects, encouraged artists to see the potential in paper pulp as a medium. This was most successfully achieved in the *Paper Pools*, 1978, by David Hockney, where Hockney revisited the imagery of the swimming pool and paintings such as *A Bigger Splash*, 1967, to make large, beautiful,

below and opposite: DIETER ROTH, *6 Piccadillies*, 1970.
Portfolio of six double-sided screenprint and photolithographs, one with iron filings, mounted on board, 48.5 x 69 cm. Courtesy Dieter Roth Estate.

TIME
BP
AIR
BEA
FREMLINS BEERS
LONG JOHN
THE BEATLES

below and opposite: DIETER ROTH, *6 Piccadillies*, 1970.
Portfolio of six double-sided screenprint and photolithographs, one with iron filings, mounted on board, 48.5 x 69 cm. Courtesy Dieter Roth Estate.

below and opposite: DIETER ROTH, *6 Piccadillies*, 1970.
Portfolio of six double-sided screenprint and photolithographs, one with iron filings, mounted on board, 48.5 x 69 cm. Courtesy Dieter Roth Estate.

BMC

below and opposite: RACHEL WHITEREAD, *B: Clapton Park Estate, Mandeville Street, London E5; Bakewell Court; Repton Court; March 1995* from *Demolished*, 1996.
Screenprints on paper, 49 x 74.5 cm. Image courtesy Charles Booth-Clibbon and The Paragon Press, London. © Rachel Whiteread.

fluid images using coloured and pressed paper pulp. This level of production, which in its complexity and use of multiple processes was on an industrial scale, was therefore costly and the prices of the prints subsequently reflected this. It was only, therefore, really viable to work with established artists who could command high prices and had international demand for their work.

On a very different level and with an intention to get ideas circulating and generate change, the Fluxus group used print and the multiple object as a way of documenting their avant-garde performances and events. Referencing Duchamp's 'readymades' and boxes, these multiples and prints were published relatively cheaply through Editions René Block in Germany, conscious of the way that a multiple image could engage and draw in an audience for their revolutionary ideas. In contrast to the scale and technical invention of the American print publishers, these editions were modest and often used commercial processes and readily available technologies. Good examples of these productions being *Weekend*, 1971, an attaché case containing an object by Joseph Beuys along with prints by, amongst others, KP Brehmer, KH Hödicke and Sigmar Polke, presented as if ready for an overnight business meeting and Marcel Broodthaers' *The Manuscript*, 1974, consisting of a bottle engraved with the title in an edition of 120, wrapped in silk paper with a printed text and contained within a box, as if a luxury gift.

The boundaries between print, the multiple and the artists' book are permeable and interlinked. For Ian Hamilton Finlay all forms of printed ephemera were a means to distribute his lyrical concrete poetry, with a large production of cards, prints and books published through his imprint, the Wild Hawthorn Press. The audience for artists' books has grown rapidly in recent years with numerous book fairs and opportunities for small publishers to make contact with their audience directly. Many of these books are hand printed in small editions and take on sculptural possibilities, through folding, construction and mixed media.

Paragon Press started modestly in 1986 with the publication of *A Scottish Bestiary* including prints by amongst others, John Bellamy, Bruce Mclean and June Redpath. Its policy of producing work in portfolios, initially focusing on British artists, helped to revive an appetite for publishing in the UK and capitalised on the interest in the young British artists or YBA's. One example being *Show and Tell*, 1996, an exquisite set of screenprints by Richard Deacon, in which, through juxtaposing the artist's photographs with his drawings, rare insights are provided into the source of his sculptural imagination. In a further example, *Demolished*, 1996, a folio by Rachel Whiteread in which she records through 12 screenprints the gradual demolition of high-rise blocks on three London estates, provides an elegant visual essay concerning her overriding interest in voids and negative space.

Many artists have used this concept of the folio or boxed set to either demonstrate the importance of series and sequence in their thinking or else to ensure that the essence of an original series can be held together in perpetuity. Donald Judd has used the series extensively to explore his interest in ideas of seriality and variation, taking simple propositions through a range of possibilities to produce work of great refinement. "Every print is an independent and separate work. But at the same time all the prints made from 1961 onwards belong to series."[13]

Roy Lichtenstein has predominantly approached printmaking as a means of exploring ideas around a particular theme, be this through genres such as the still life, interiors or as meditations on a single motif as in the facade study of *Rouen Cathedral*, 1969. Writing candidly, he states that he liked the "activity of deciding to do a group of prints. I don't particularly like the activity of doing one print. It just interrupts my focus."[14]

His series such as *Cathedrals*, 1969, *Haystacks*, 1969, *Mirrors*, 1969, and *Bull Profile*, 1973, are essential when assessing his work, revealing both a working method and the graphic sensibility that underpins all his work.

The Alan Cristea Gallery has been important in advancing the acceptance of digital prints within the overall tradition of printmaking. For over 30 years, Alan Cristea has published many of the leading international artists alongside representing modern masters. He has been alert to the changing nature of print and the new opportunities available to his artists, Michael Craig-Martin and Julian Opie being just two who have taken advantage of this.

Digital technology has brought into question what might constitute a print, the inkjet print being only one solution. Craig-Martin in recent work such as *Coming*, 2006, has used the flat LCD screen as the surface for an image in which his vector drawings, controlled through bespoke software on a customised computer, ebb and flow in a continuingly changing configuration. Julian Opie has experimented with a variety of solutions many of which take the representation of movement as their subject. This has led to works that function as animations on screen through to large-scale lenticular prints of figures that appear to move in relationship to the viewer. Very differently, Terry Winters has used digital technology to drive lasers to cut his woodblocks, the results combining the mechanically precise line with the physical surface qualities of woodcut. In contrast Damien Hirst, in his series of 13 screenprints, *The Last Supper*, 1999, makes apparent the modern artists' studio. Typography, layout, colour management and the final artwork are all performed within a digital environment under Hirst's direction.

The contemporary scene for printmaking is as wide and varied as it is possible to imagine. While in one direction, as already mentioned, artists have been keen to explore some of the advanced technological opportunities, there has also been a movement back to very simply direct forms of print. Tracey Emin revisits the monotype and uses this simple transfer method to give her drawings a nervous edgy quality. This direct uncomplicated approach also underpins the stencil graffiti work of the urban artist Banksy whose work can be seen in various locations, most abundantly in Bristol. In his case, given the subversive nature of his street art, his limited edition prints are surprisingly conventional, taking on the characteristics of mainstream printmaking. While Emin and Banksy have sought an uncomplicated approach to monotype, Mick Moon has found in the process a method more akin to painting, with complex surfaces built up from overprinting richly textured blocks.

From the monotype at one extreme and experiments in digital imaging at the other, one distinct feature of the contemporary scene is that prints have become ubiquitous. Furthermore, they do not necessarily have to announce themselves as prints or require being separated into a distinct category.

Increasingly, prints feature alongside paintings and sculptures and within or as installations. This was well illustrated when Simon Patterson presented his lithograph, *The Great Bear*, 1992, a reworking of the London underground map, as part of his exhibition at Tate Britain in 1996 for the Turner Prize shortlist. The work was received with hardly a reference to its being a print, it was simply accepted as a key work in this artist's œuvre. Conversely in the Tallinn Print Triennial in 2007, the major prize was awarded to the Columbian artist Oscar Muños for his *Project for a Memorial*, 2005, a multi-screen video projection which eloquently spoke of loss and memory. In this work, faces of people, repeatedly painted on to stone, slowly vanish, as if their only salvation was through this continuous act of remembrance and picturing.

While these changes are to be welcomed, there are many that would draw a division between those artists who make their own prints and those who engage the services of professional printers. These tensions find their expression in print competitions, awards and biennials where occasionally a demonstration of fine technique can take precedent over content. A number of open print exhibitions have revisited their submission procedures, allowing for work which breaks with the convention of the single, moderately sized print on paper. In the Ljubljana Biennial of Graphic Arts, the process of inviting curators to each select work has not only given the event a critical edge but has resulted in a wide range of approaches to print to be seen. The work shown has been challenging, placing, for example, the installations and expanded practice of the Italian artist Massimo Bartolini, or the suspended printed dresses of the Slovenian artists Marija Staric and Almira Sadar, within a broad context of printmaking.

Largely through the impact of new technology, print has been able to escape from the frame and move out of the gallery. Projects to put artworks on beer bottles, wing tails of aeroplanes, carrier bags, cakes and as a part of architecture are just some of the ways printmaking has become an expanded practice. The possibilities for prints can be seen developing in 3-D as rapid prototyping and 3-D colour printers become more available and in works which will be made in virtual reality. Meanwhile haptic technology offers opportunities to produce works, which can be experienced physically in virtual reality allowing for the sense of touch, (still a taboo) to be part of the viewer's experience.

It is perhaps fitting to end with the Chinese artist Wenda Gu whose installation *Forest of Stone Steles—Retranslation & Rewriting of Tang Poetry*, 1993–2005, was first shown at the Contemporary Art Center of He Xiangning Art Museum in China in 2005. Gu presented 50 stone blocks each weighing over a tonne. On each block was a Tang poem, which was the subject of translation from Chinese characters, into English, back into Chinese, and then again into English to show how meaning is changed and transformed through the act of translation. The resulting texts cut into the stone blocks by craftsman were then printed through direct rubbing, as with the very earliest prints, to produce printed texts, which surround the formal installation of the stones. The installation in essence presents both the prints as well as their matrix in a complex but poetic exploration of what it is to attempt to communicate; what is lost and what is gained. I would also propose that it eloquently speaks of the role of print, its importance across time and cultures and its essential role in this most human of needs.

SIMON PATTERSON, *The Great Bear*, 1992.
Lithograph on paper, four-colour lithograph in glass and aluminium frame, 109 x 134.5 cm, edition of 50. Photo by Stephen White. Courtesy Haunch of Venison. © Simon Patterson and Transport for London.

WENDA GU, *Forest of Stone Steles—Retranslation & Rewriting of Tang Poetry*, 1993–2005.
Ink rubbings, stone carving studio, Xi'an, China, 110 cm x 190 cm x 20 cm. Courtesy the artist and Art Gallery of the University of North Texas, USA.

WENDA GU, *Forest of Stone Steles—Retranslation & Rewriting of Tang Poetry*, 1993–2005.
Ink rubbings, stone carving studio, Xi'an, China, 110 cm x 190 cm x 20 cm, 1.3 tones each. Photo by Ya Niu. Courtesy the artist and Oct Contemporary Art Center, He Xiangning Art Museum, Shenzhen, China, Collection of The Museum of Modern Art, New York.

REW
TRA

LUCIAN FREUD, *Girl with Fuzzy Hair*, 2004.
Etching, 63.5 x 50 cm, edition of 46. Courtesy Lucian Freud Archive. © Lucian Freud 2004.

ORKING DITIONS

As is readily apparent, there are artists who have established themselves within the history of printmaking as innovators, bringing radically new approaches to bear on the tradition, but equally there are those artists that sit within a tradition and explore their vision through established conventions. Lucian Freud is one such artist who has developed a powerful body of work using little more than direct drawing through an etching ground.

> When (Graham) Sutherland gave Freud his etching tools and told him to look more thoroughly into the technical craft of etching, this discouraged rather than encouraged the young artist. Freud was not interested in what he saw as the mystical paraphernalia of the etching craft; he was interested in it as a spontaneous drawing medium, which he could etch—"One dip. Really quick and dangerous"—in the nearest available basin.[1]

While these prints can be seen as accepting the conventions of etching, it is through the uncompromising vision and insightful line that raise these prints on to a level that makes them amongst the most compelling images of their generation. They further engender a particular relationship with the edge of the plate, evoking the accidental cropping or formal central framing devices of photography. The convention of the printed image framed within a single sheet, is an ideal format for emphasising the physical nature of the edge, in Freud's case, an aperture through which to see the world.

While Freud has been able to find the simple etched line sufficient, for Paula Rego it is the possibilities offered through aquatint that has been the bedrock of her engagement with print. Working within the tradition of Goya, her printmaking has remained remarkably conventional, a convenient cover for her dark and subversive images. Her use of aquatint is masterful, working from the lightest through to the darkest tones, but all the time ensuring that the function of technique is to carry the idea and not be subsumed by it. In this way, for all their elegance, there is awkwardness; a jarring that brings the image to the fore. For Rego, each print is a painting in miniature and it is through this medium that she has realised many of her most compelling and memorable images. It is also through printmaking that she connects with the narrative tradition of storytelling and children's illustration that is fundamental to an understanding of her work. While her paintings and pastels have grown increasingly complex and are the result of long periods of work, prints can be made more quickly ensuring that there is an output for her flow of stories. "Rego finds printmaking extremely satisfying, not only as an antidote to painting, but as a means by which images may flow thick and fast from her mind."[2]

This was certainly the case in the outpouring of images, over 35 prints made within a period of four to five months that resulted in the series of *Nursery Rhymes*, 1989. This series established Rego as a leading figure within printmaking, working initially with intaglio but in more recent years producing substantial work through lithography as in her prints for *Jane Eyre*, 2002. An example of the way Rego has developed her imagery through etching is well illustrated in the progressive states for *The Wild Duck*, 1990.

PAULA REGO, *The Wild Duck*, proof states and final print, 1990.
Etching and aquatint, paper 60.5 x 50 cm / image 29.5 x 24 cm, edition of 75. Published by the National Art Collections Fund in 1990. Courtesy of Marlborough Fine Art (London) Ltd.

PAULA REGO, *Polly put the kettle on* from the series *The Nursery Rhymes*, 1989.
Etching and aquatint, paper 52 x 38 cm / image 21.5 x 22.5 cm, edition of 50. Published by the artist and Marlborough Graphics in 1989. Courtesy of Marlborough Fine Art (London) Ltd.

Known principally as a maker of extraordinary pots that subvert ceramic's polite history, Grayson Perry has turned to the tradition of printed maps in his forays into printing. *Print for a Politician*, 2005, operates somewhere between a map and a painting by Pieter Bruegel the Younger, the map both suggesting an aerial view of an imagined landscape, and a narrative, full of detail and observation. The inventiveness in Perry's approach to print lies within his need to explore imagery rather than technical innovation. In fact it is the tension between the familiar style and authority within the print and the transgressive subject matter that gives these works their edge.

Emma Stibbon also takes landscape as her source; in her case it is the romantic and sublime landscape of abandoned or distant places. These are places seen and remembered as apposed to imagined. "I want to describe places that put a perspective on the viewer. Although the work is linked to the topographical, observed place, I want to reach a sort of psychological state, a kind of emotional equivalence."[3]

She takes the wood itself as an expressive element and uses the grain of the wood as a counterpoint to the drawn passages. The success of these prints lies in this balance between control and improvisation, between what is drawn and what is given by the medium.

There has been a resurgence of interest in woodcut; it offers the contemporary artist the potential to work at a large scale, at little cost and since it can be printed by hand, to make prints on a scale which can go beyond any size restriction that a press would impose.

Christiane Baumgartner, a German artist from Leipzig, a city steeped in the tradition of print, uses the old medium of woodcut to reflect on the modern world as mediated through TV and video. Like Stibbon, Baumgartner's landscapes are deserted, but for her these are moments frozen and captured in an instant. Her landscapes show the evidence of man, wind farms on a hill, cars on motorways, a road lined by trees, all rendered through a matrix of horizontal lines acting as the equivalent of the TV screen. They hover between static and fleeting, passing images, like scenes from films half remembered. The viewer is compelled to oscillate between the implied space of the image presented and the assertion of the image's flatness, compounded by the technique itself that only records surface information. Jeremy Lewison suggests that "to be detached is to protect oneself from giving away information that might be used against you. Ordinariness is the vehicle for secret communication and Baumgartner's images have the look of the ordinary while being far from it."[4]

Katsutoshi Yuasa also uses woodcut to reinterpret photographs, rendering the illusion of tone through the subtle cutting of the block. Yuasa's prints can be read at a distance but gradually dissolve as they are approached, disintegrating into abstraction and marks. He says that; "After spending several weeks carving on plywood and printing on paper, the work as a final result of my representation is already far away from the original, simultaneously it is not reality or fiction."[5] While Baumgartner references back to a German graphic tradition, Yuasa draws on Japanese printmaking with its attention to nature, detail and pattern.

top: GRAYSON PERRY, *Print for a Politician*, 2005.
Etching from three plates, 67 x 249.5 cm. Printed by Stoneman Graphics. Courtesy Grayson Perry, Victoria Miro Gallery and The Paragon Press, London.

bottom: EMMA STIBBON, *Abandoned Whaling Station, Deception Island*, 2006.
Woodcut, 117 x 238 cm. Photo by Stuart Bunce. Courtesy the artist.

CHRISTIANE BAUMGARTNER, *Allee I + II*, 2008.
Diptych woodcut on Kozo paper, 142 x 181 cm each, edition of six. Printed by the artist, Leipzig. Distributed by Johan Deumens, Haarlem and Alan Cristea Gallery, London. Courtesy Christiane Baumgartner and Alan Cristea Gallery, London. © DACS 2009.

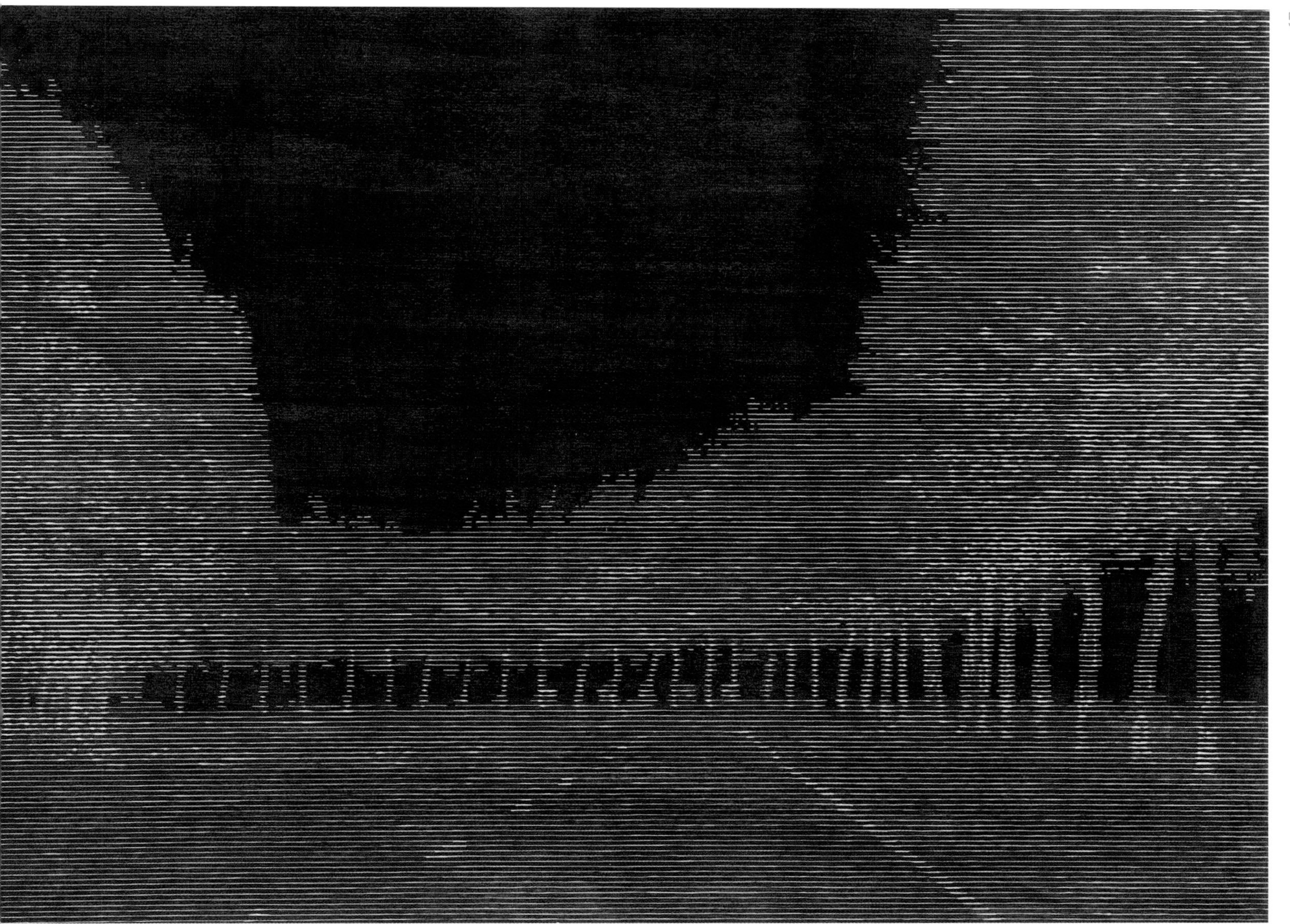

KATSUTOSHI YUASA, *A Place where there is no redemption and no apocalypse # 1*, 2008.
Lithographic ink woodcut on Laurier 100% cotton fine art paper, 163 x 120 cm, edition of five.
Courtesy the artist and TAG Fine Arts.

KATSUTOSHI YUASA, *Echoes*, 2008.
Lithographic ink woodcut on BFK Rives 100% cotton fine art paper, 122 x 244 cm, edition of five. Courtesy the artist and TAG Fine Arts.

VIJA CELMINS, *Ocean Surface*, 1992.
Woodcut, paper 50 x 40 cm / image 22.5 x 30.5 cm. Published by Greenfell Press, New York.
Courtesy the artist and McKee Gallery.

The photograph itself becomes the subject for Vija Celmins who has used the processes of woodcut and mezzotint to build images of the sea or the night sky with painstaking attention to the subtlest nuance. It feels as if the very slowness of these traditional processes, mezzotint being particularly laborious, is in stark contrast to the instant nature of the photograph. In reference to her woodcut, *Ocean Surface*, 1992, Celmins describes her fascination with the process:

> my work has always been so involved in the 'physical' that cutting into the wood with this little knife was very satisfying. I lived for months with my face inches away from the block, cutting this way and that. I never really had a technique... just trying to build a solid piece that could hold still and move at the same time. When you come very close to the print I think you feel the touch of the knife.[6]

This concentrated energy at the very surface of the print, draws the viewer to share in Celmin's painstaking act of reconstruction. Seung Yeon Kim, likewise, looks back to these slow processes. Mezzotint, with its capacity to render rich deep dark tones becomes the chosen medium for Kim's cityscapes of Seoul. While often used to evoke natural landscapes, mezzotint is less associated with rendering the modern city. These images go beyond mere topographical evidence as through the action of slowly burnishing the plate, proceeding from a starting point of pitch black, he literally illuminates the view, turning on the streetlights and neon signs to reveal the city at night.

Tony Bevan is an artist who has consistently focused on the motif of the single head, in many cases his own, as a recurring theme in his work.

> As the most immediately recognisable to us all—going back to one's infancy, with the comforting presences of the looming fractures of one's parents and siblings—the face is also the motif with which the greatest liberties can be taken without becoming indecipherable or losing identity.[7]

He simultaneously parallels the struggle to capture an image conceptually, with the physical effort to cut the wood for his woodcuts as in *Head*, 1994, or engrave the metal plates in his drypoints. In *Portrait Head*, in opposition to the received wisdom of pulling the drypoint needle to create a sinuous line, Bevan uses drypoint to create thick lines composed of multiple scars raised up on the surface to hold the maximum amount of ink. In turn they present a challenge to the eye, a resistance to the otherwise fluidity of the drawing. Likewise, in his woodcuts, echoing Edvard Munch's approach, whole areas are left uncut, as the grain itself acts as an expressive surface in contrast to the drawing, which literally gouges a path through the wood.

top: SEUNG YEON KIM, *Night Landscape—20062*, 2007.
Mezzotint, 40 x 60 cm. Courtesy the artist.
bottom: SEUNG YEON KIM, *Night Landscape—20082*, 2007.
Mezzotint, 30 x 60 cm. Courtesy the artist.

ROBIN DUTTSON, *Multi Apple Blossom I*, 2007.
Linocut on Seikosen paper, 91 x 66 cm, edition of 30. Courtesy the artist and TAG Fine Arts.

TONY BEVAN, *Head*, 1994.
Woodcut on paper, Croindene Press, 53 x 73 cm. Courtesy the artist.

Linoleum, a softer material than wood, offers less resistance to the artist's hand. The material allows for a fluid, flowing line, a quality that Robin Duttson exploits in his large relief prints. Printed in subdued colours, they reference back to Japanese woodcuts of blossoms and flowers, but are charged with a contemporary sense of objective research.

As with Duttson, the Japanese *ukiyo-e* tradition also provide fertile territory for Masami Teraoka who looks to this for both style and the subject matter of fantasy, pleasure and the senses. He ups the scale and in these large-format prints, focuses on contemporary scenes, both quoting directly from the past while infusing it with a cryptic take on modern life and eroticism.

> I often wish my *sensei* (teacher) Utagawa Kunisada (1786–1865) were alive. I would love to see how and what he would draw in America. I depict a fantasy scene of Kunisada in Hawaii watching the solar eclipse. His view is obscured by the sight of an American woman who diverts his attention, changing his sightseeing plans, as well as eclipsing the eclipse.[8]

The scale of many of these prints bring into sharp focus the tradition of multiblock printing combining a beautiful line with the technique of gradated blended colour. However, these prints of Teraoka were made with a combination of processes, bringing together under the direction of Ken Tyler, etching, screenprint and woodblocks. The images suggest a collision of cultures, highlighting real political and social issues such as AIDS and child abuse.

Nana Shiomi, an artist originally from Japan now working in London, also looks back to the *ukiyo-e* tradition for a schematised representation of space. Quoting directly from, amongst others, Katsushika Hokusai, Paul Cézanne and Marcel Duchamp, she brings together references from both East and West in these elegantly realised prints. Many of the prints take the form of diptyches, each side offering a reflection of the other, while her epic series *One Hundred Views of MITATE*, 1998, offer a space defined by receding floorboards, into which a myriad of objects and characters enter. She defines MITATE as being "a fundamental concept in all Japanese art from the earliest time. Basically, MITATE involves a substitution of the intended subject by something simpler and vaguer."[9]

MASAMI TERAOKA, *AIDS Series/Geisha in Bath*, 2008.
A woodblock print in 46 colours from 34 blocks of carved, laminated cherry wood, paper 52 x 32.5 cm / image 46.5 x 32.5 cm, edition of 200 plus proofs. Printed by Satoshi Hishimura on Echizen Kizuki Hosho, 100% Kozo paper by Ichibe Iwano who bears the title National Living Treasure. Blocks carved by Motoharu Aasaka. Courtesy the artist and Catharine Clark Gallery, San Francisco, USA.

MASAMI TERAOKA, *Hawaii Snorkel Series/Longing Samurai*, 1993.
24-colour woodcut, etching and aquatint printed from one copper plate and 11 woodblocks on natural Fuji handmade paper, paper and image 65 x 97 cm, edition of 30 plus 18 proofs. Printed and proofed by Anthony Kirk, Susan Hover, Kenneth Tyler, and Paul Stillpass. Woodblock preparation, carving and printing by Yasuyuki Shibata. Published by Tyler Graphics, Mount Kisco, New York, with its chop mark in the paper. Courtesy the artist and Catharine Clark Gallery, San Francisco, USA.

NANA SHIOMI, *Book of Five Elements*, 1999.
Woodcut Print with water-based inks, paper 63 x 90 cm / image 51 x 80 cm, edition of 30.
Printed by Baren. Courtesy the artist.

NANA SHIOMI, *No.12, Flower* from *One Hundred Views of MITATE*, 1998.
Woodcut Print with water-based inks, printed by Baren, paper 46 x 46 cm / image 34 x 34 cm, edition of ten. Printed by Baren. Courtesy the artist.

PA
APPR

NTERLY

OACHES

Printmaking processes can engender a degree of separation from the immediacy of painting. There is an intermediary, a surface or material to be worked which then forms the matrix from which the print is drawn. How can the artist bridge this gap and give their prints a physical presence and an equivalence to a painterly surface? This chapter looks at some of the ways painters have approached this issue, from Sean Scully's rich overlays of aquatint to Howard Hodgkin's prints with hand-colouring and Antoni Tàpies use of carborundum and embossing.

Whilst printmaking and painting can be seen as close bedfellows, printmaking requires the artist to work through a process and through the material of the matrix itself, the etching plate, the lithographic stone or the woodblock. In addition, particularly when working with colour, there is a translation required between the mark made and the realisation of that mark as a printed image. Painters have adopted a number of very different strategies in resolving these issues and ensuring that their prints retains the immediacy of their paintings.

Anselm Kiefer's work combines painting, sculpture, photography, and printmaking. In his monumental woodcuts such as *Der Rhein, 1983,* and *Wege der Weltweisheit: Die Hermannsschlacht*, 1978, woodcut is used as a starting point in the making of an image. Individual prints are pasted together to form these works which stand alongside his paintings in terms of physical presence. In fact to even call these works prints is to mislead. They are collages formed from prints, each separate woodcut hand-printed then used as material in the final work. The woodcuts are unevenly inked with the character of trial proofs left on the studio floor. Having been pasted together, they are then the subject of further transgressions as Kiefer, works on top of the prints with shellac and other materials. The resulting images, made over time are about time itself, time passing and time remembered.

Kiefer uses print as opposed to making prints. He uses print for its intrinsic graphic quality and for the fact that, like a photograph, a print carries with it an air of authority.

In stark contrast, Prunella Clough made her own prints as well as using the services of professional studios. Her monotypes, lithographs and etchings are on a modest scale, often balancing one or two elements to create images of deceptive elegance and poise. They are made with the sensuous eye of the painter pushing and pulling the forms to create a tension between those shapes made and those implied.

While Clough's prints explore the flatness of print, Howard Hodgkin has sought equivalents to the layering process in painting. He has developed prints which transpose the feeling of painting with a loaded brush into a graphic language. Working with the master printer Jack Sheriff, he has combined the techniques of sugar-lift aquatint with carborundum printing, both processes allowing the artist to translate the immediacy of the brush stroke into a printable surface. In carborundum printing, carborundum powder is mixed with a glue to form a paste which can then be painted directly on to a plate and, when dry, will form a textured surface which can be inked up and printed. Hodgkin's prints are built up through layers of colour, creating both depth and a rich interplay of forms. To further endorse the painterly mark, Hodgkin often incorporates elaborate hand-colouring into the process, not to colour in but to act as a counterpoint to the printed elements.

> **The hand-colouring in Hodgkin's prints varies from edition to edition. Sometimes it is used as a bottom layer, primarily to colour the paper. Sometimes it is sandwiched between different printed runs through the press. At other times it is applied after the print run is complete.... It has brought to many of his prints the *alla prima* quality and vividness of surface found in his paintings.**[1]

The signature blocks of colour that are immediately recognisable as the work of Sean Scully have provided rich opportunities for exploring these ideas through printmaking. Scully, rather than combining processes, explores his imagery through a singular process, be it etching, woodcut or lithography. Each medium engenders a particular approach, the sharp differentiation as can be seen in his woodcuts, contrasts to the almost calligraphic feel that he achieves through lithography and the sensuous liquidity of his aquatints. His approach to printmaking suggests the sensibility of a composer, aware of the range of each instrument, but testing each to reveal their intrinsic character. Whilst Scully asserts the physicality of his blocks of colour, Hwajin Chang creates skeins of colour through combining lithography and screenprint, suggesting a cultural layering, which both conceals and reveals. In *Low Culture*, 1987, the image

ANSELM KIEFER, *Der Rhein*, 1983.
Woodcut with oil, acrylic and shellac, mounted on canvas, 280 x 280 cm. Image courtesy White Cube. © Anselm Kiefer.

PRUNELLA CLOUGH, *Untitled*, circa 1964.
Monotype and collage, 37.5 x 31.5 cm. Image courtesy Flowers London. © Prunella Clough (1919–1999), © Estate of Prunella Clough 2009, all rights reserved DACS.

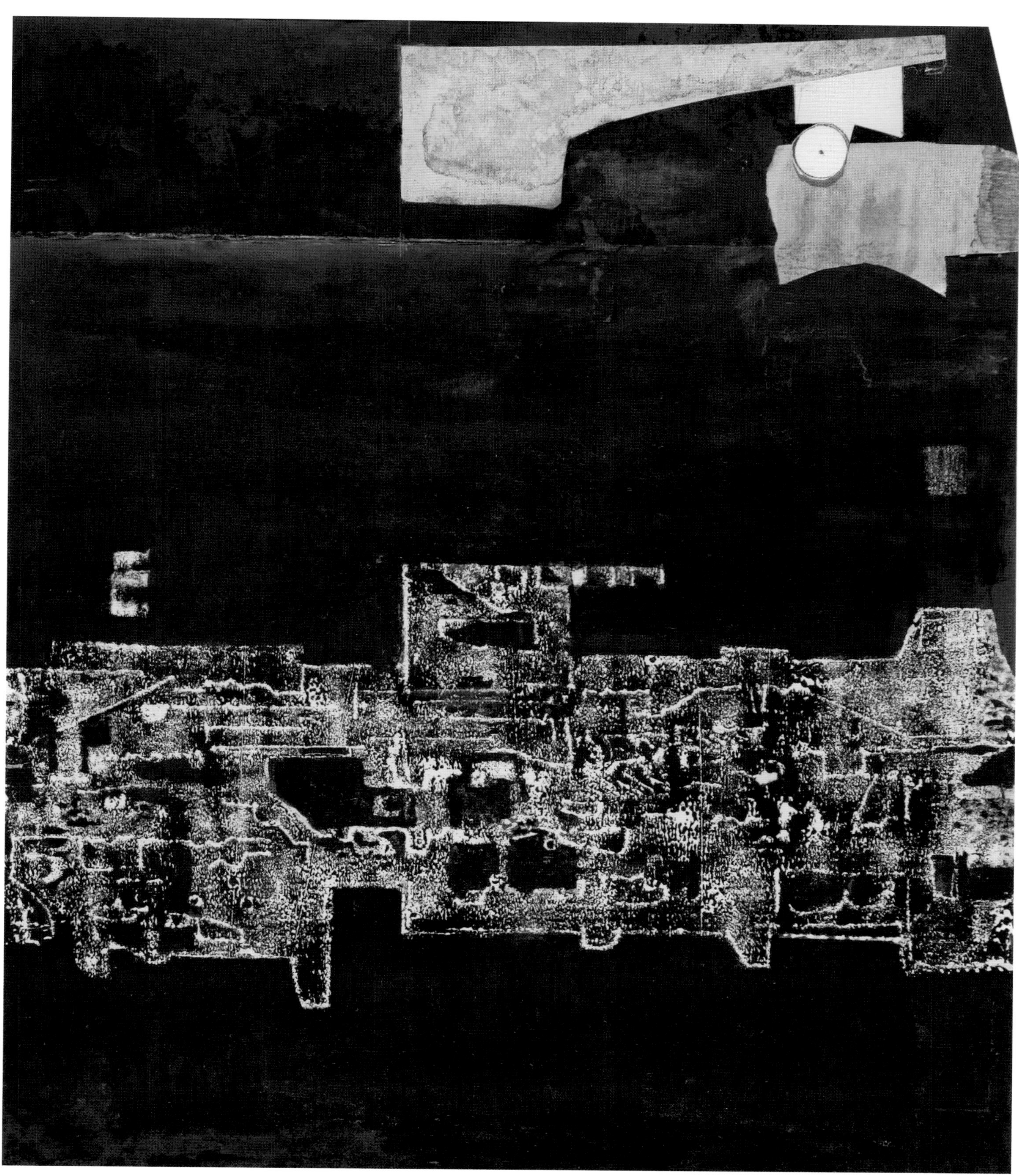

HOWARD HODGKIN, *Venice, Evening*, 1995.
16 part hand-painted etching and aquatint with carborundum, printed from five plates on Velin arches blanc 300 gsm paper, overall paper size 160 x 196.5 cm, edition of 60. Printed at 107 Workshop, Wiltshire. Published by Alan Cristea Gallery, London. Courtesy Howard Hodgkin and Alan Cristea Gallery, London.

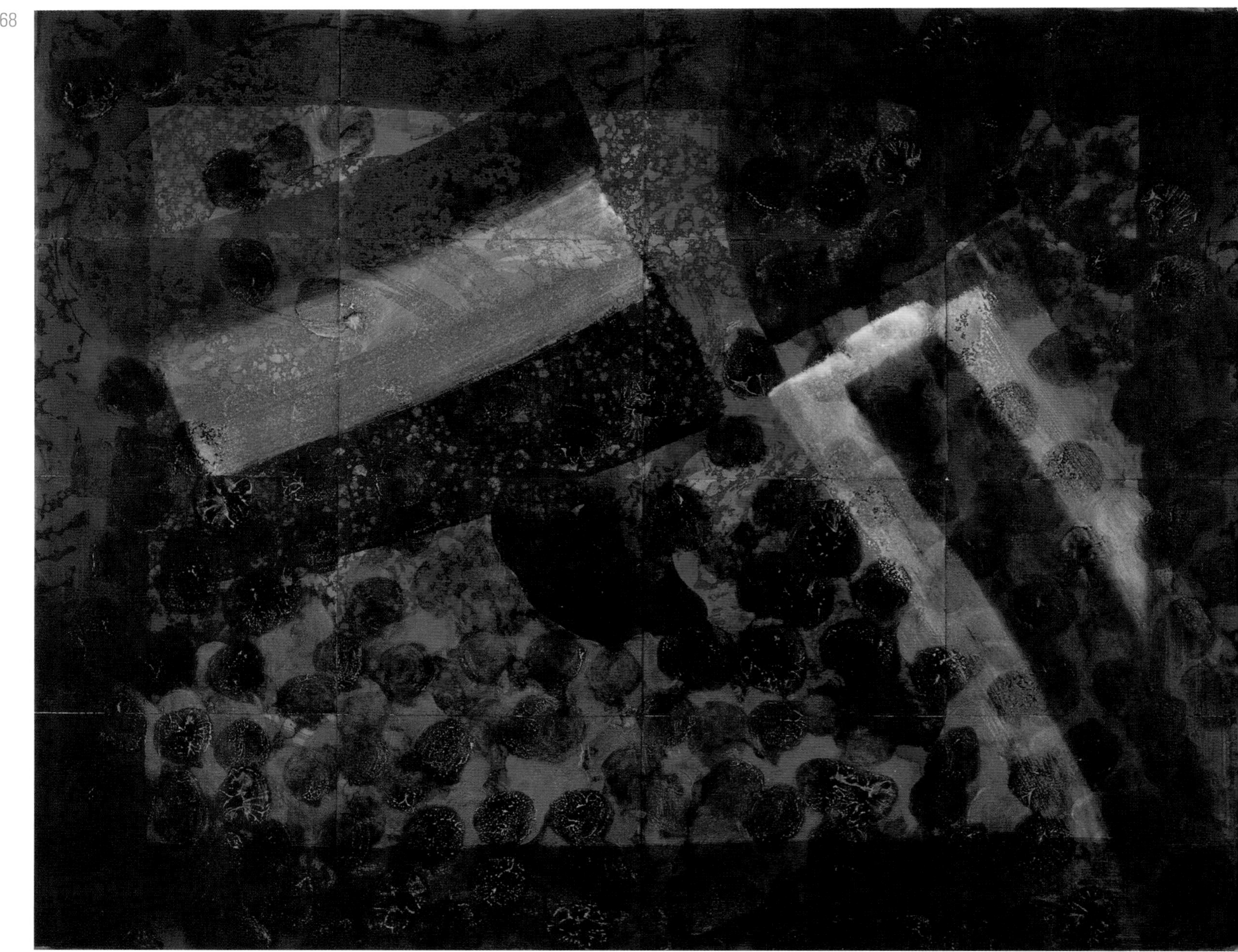

top: SEAN SCULLY, *Barcelona Day*, 2005.
Aquatint, printed on Arches 300 gsm, paper 68.5 x 80 cm / image 39.5 x 54.5 cm, edition of 40. Printed at Ignasi Aguirre, Barcelona. Published by Galeria Carles Tache, Barcelona. Courtesy the artist.

bottom: SEAN SCULLY, *π*, 1994.
Etching, spitbite, sugar-lift and aquatint, printed on Somerset textured white, paper 60 x 80 cm / image 40.5 x 51 cm, edition of 98. Printed by Jennifer Melby, Munich. Published by Galerie Bernd Klüser, Munich. Courtesy the artist.

HWAJIN CHANG, *Low Culture*, 1989.
Lithograph, silkscreen, 59 x 96 cm. Courtesy the artist.

HWAJIN CHANG, *Low Culture II*, 1998.
Lithograph, polyester sticker, 60 x 89 cm. Courtesy the artist.

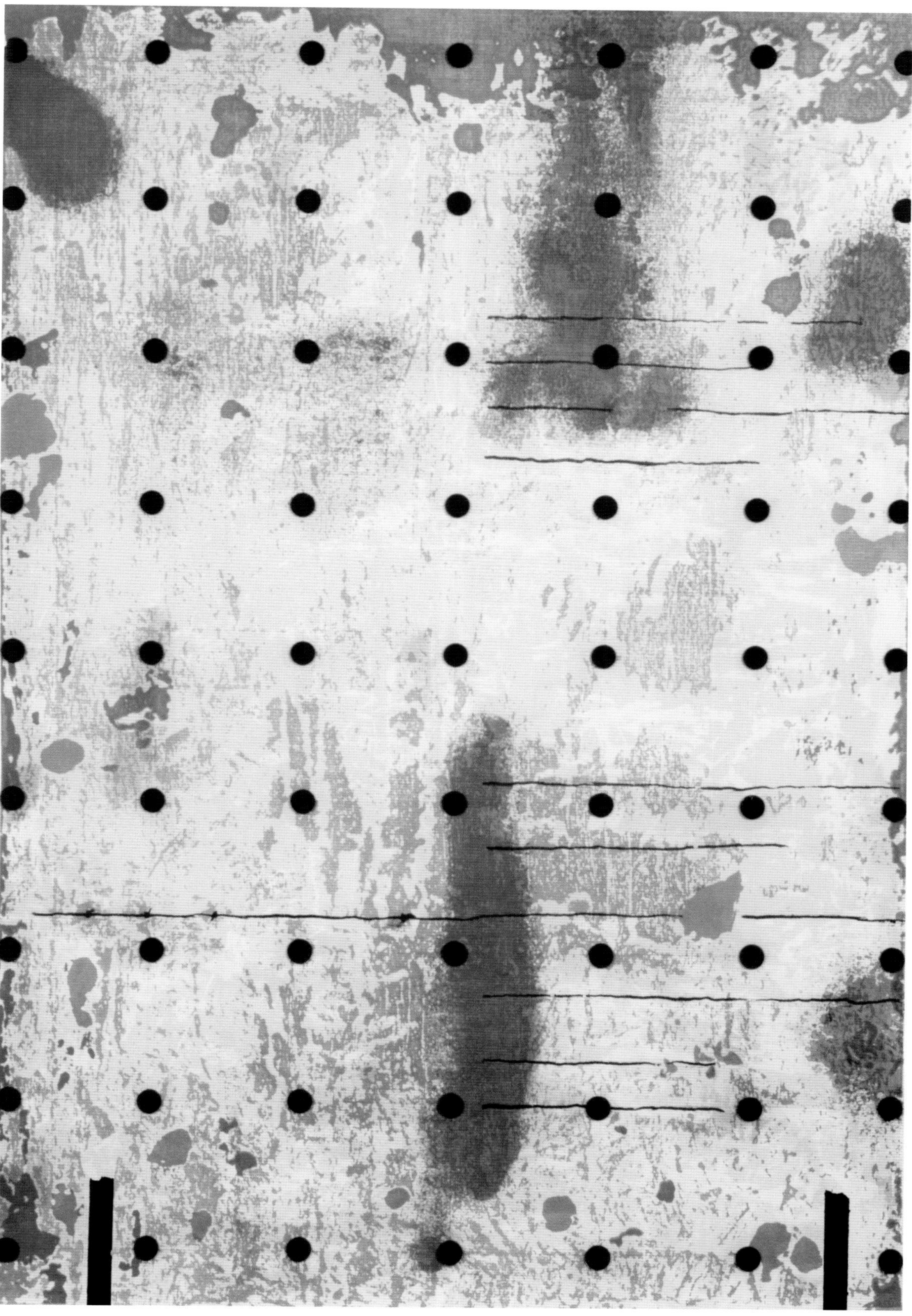

BERNARD COHEN, *Things Seen II*, 2005.
Etching and aquatint, 78.5 x 92.5 cm, edition of 30. Printed by Shark's Ink. Published by Flowers London. Courtesy the artist and Flowers London. © Bernard Cohen.

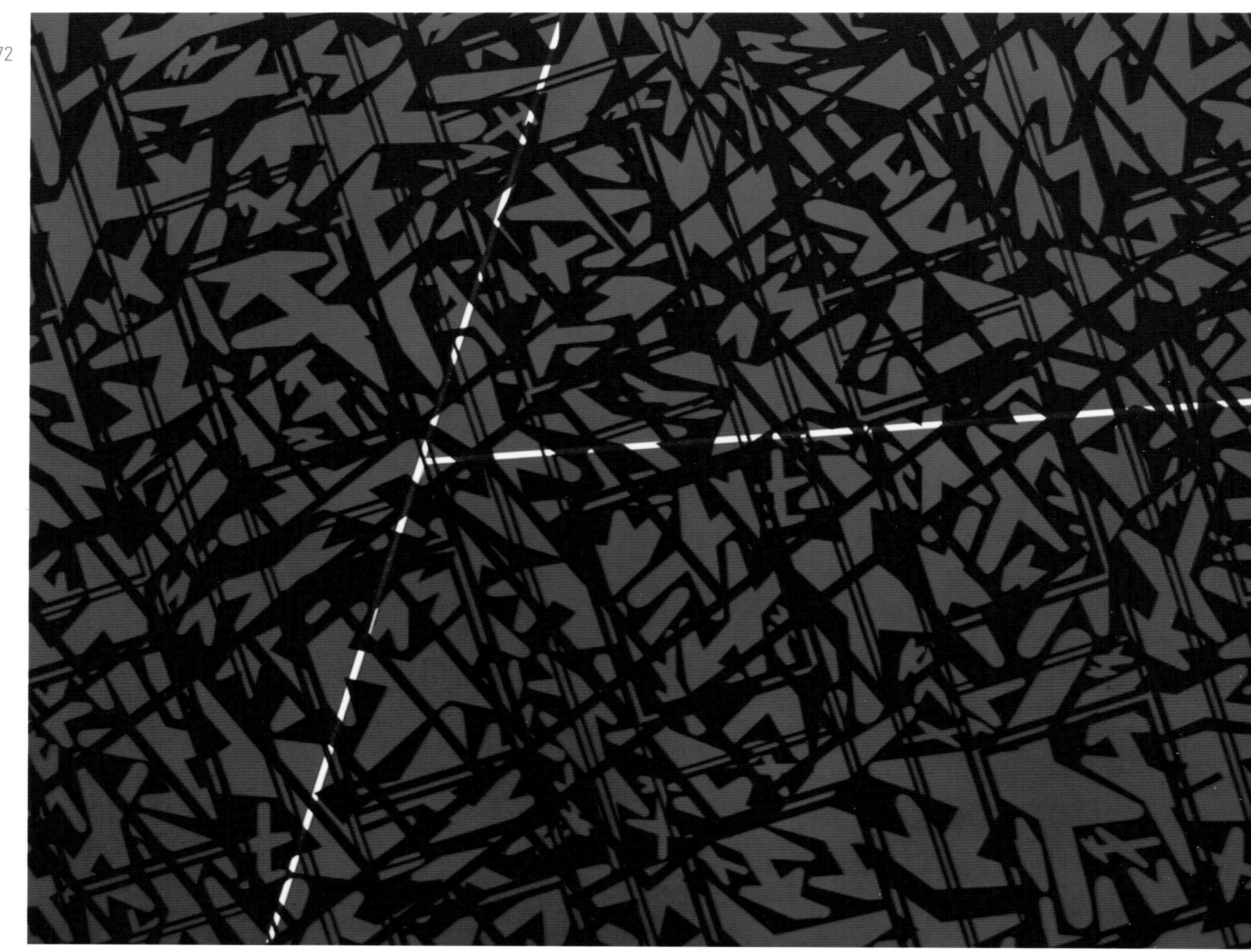

ANTONI TÀPIES, *Novel·la*, 1965.
31 lithographs by Antoni Tàpies, text by Joan Brossa, Vitella Guarro paper, made especially for this work with a 'Sala Gaspar' filigree, paper 39 x 28.5 cm and 39 x 57 cm / book 39.5 x 28.5 cm. Image courtesy Galeria Toni Tàpies. © Foundation Antoni Tàpies, Barcelone/VEGAP, Madrid and DACS, London 2009.

is divided, drawing attention to the intersection with the dark screened layer and the layer below, offering just enough evidence for the viewer to retrace the artist's decisions.

A sense of layering is pre-eminent in both the paintings and prints of Bernard Cohen. In his prints complex webs of line and colour seem to trap forms, acting like pauses within the action. Within a distinct abstract language, Cohen's work alludes to play, social interaction and ritual. The meal seems to be a recurring theme, the dining table as a stage of exchange and discourse. His prints draw upon a rich and inventive repertoire of shapes and stencils, made memorable through his idiosyncratic use of colour. A further strength in these prints is the manner in which they show Cohen's understanding of the subtle nature of colour lithography, in their use of relatively few colours and working with the inherent transparency of the inks, to create images that give the impression of a full palette. This is achieved through Cohen's subtle juxtaposition of colour, the use of overprinting and using the white of the paper as a colour in itself.

While Cohen's colour is bright active and celebratory, Tàpies uses colour as material, mixing browns, greys and blacks as the equivalents of the surfaces of plaster and stone. Like walls in old cities that record histories through erosion, graffiti, scrawled gestures, letters and numbers, his images reveal the trace of the human presence. As in his paintings, characterised by their impasto surfaces and combination of real and drawn elements, his prints draw the viewer to the surface and often include embossed elements or impressions of actual clothing, as in *Camisa*, 1972.

> **Tàpies has worked continuously with lithography and intaglio. Adding the collograph technique, carborundum, flocking and traditional collage, he often builds a sculptural relief on traditionally flat surfaces, developing a remarkable tactility that corresponds to his work in painting and appeals to the fingertips as well as to the eyes.**[2]

Tàpies has worked with a number of poets including Joan Brossa on collaborative projects for bookworks and folios of prints. These question the distinction between text and image and, in doing so, reference back to the Oriental tradition of the relationship between the calligraphic mark and poetry itself. These books are striking in their physicality and are an extension to his graphic work. It is difficult to underestimate the influence of Tàpies on subsequent generations of printmakers. His prints, in their degree of experimentation, challenge the conventions of what is permissible, while also demonstrating a remarkable sophistication and control of process.

Printmaking in all its forms has been a rich territory for the artist Christopher Le Brun ranging from small scale etchings measuring under 7 x 13 cm through to large monotypes made at the Garner Tullis Print workshop, in Santa Barbara, California, one of which composed of 60 sections finally measured over 450 x 1,100 cm. He has used print to explore his range of motifs, hovering between

CHRISTOPHER LE BRUN, *Four Riders*, 1993.
Four etchings numbered LI–LIV, 58 x 57 cm, edition of 30 plus eight artist's proofs.
Courtesy Christopher Le Brun and The Paragon Press, London.

TRENTON DOYLE HANCOCK, *Fix*, 2007.
A portfolio of 20 pages, utilising combinations of etching, lithography and silkscreen, 35.5 x 35.5 cm, edition of 30. Printed by Randy Hemminghaus. Published by the Brodsky Center for Innovative Editions. Image courtesy the artist and the Brodsky Center for Innovative Editions.

figuration and abstraction as well as the opportunities for chance and surprise. Many of his ventures into printmaking have resulted in series of works including two major suites in 1990 and 2005, both comprising of 50 small scale etchings. They preserve a feeling of spontaneity, with some plates having the immediacy of drawing while others are more worked up as if small paintings. In another series, *Four Riders*, 1993, Le Brun takes full advantage of the fact that an etching plate can produce, not only multiple impressions of a single image, but can also serve as a starting point for a totally new image. Here, plates are reworked, reconfigured and used to explore the progression of an idea, each image carrying the ghost of the previous stage.

> Le Brun's painting and etching now relate to one another in complex ways; ideas generated in his paintings and later reintroduced into subsequent etchings. In a sense he uses etching in the same way that some artists use drawing, formulating his ideas in the medium.[3]

Trenton Doyle Hancock takes an imagined story of "the Mounds", a set of mythical characters that seem to bring together Phillip Guston's brooding protagonists, the surrealism of the Chapman brothers with the colour and imagination of Marvel comics. In a beautiful and inventive set of multimedia prints made at the The Brodsky Center for Innovative Editions, *Fix*, 2007, he takes these characters through their paces. And while the images are small in scale, measuring just 35 cm square, they have a monumentality and, through the combination of processes, an intense feeling of discovery.

While for Le Brun and Hancock, printmaking offers the opportunity to conjure up and discover imagery, Chuck Close takes the process of printmaking as a means to interrogate his signature portraits but as Richard Shiff notes:

> the sources for Close's painted portraits are not his models but their photographs. Printmaking adds another transformation to the relationship established between painting and photography.... Each visit back to a given face (already represented at least once) translates into a new experience of making, destabilising what has been fixed.[4]

Close has taken his concerns into a range of processes including etching, mezzotint, screenprint, lithography, woodcut and graphic works made with paper pulp. In each case there is a dialogue or perhaps in some cases a battle, between the image and the quality of the process adopted. It is as if the process becomes the filter through which the image is interrogated. His first print as a professional artist set the agenda for future projects. In *Keith/Mezzotint*, 1972, he deliberately chose to work with mezzotint, a particularly labour intensive and demanding process more associated with the eighteenth century than contemporary art. To further ratchet up the demands both on himself and those working with him at Crown Point Press, his decision to work on such a large scale, (a plate size of 112 x 89 cm) required a new press to accommodate the project. The finished print has an eerie quality, close up, the squared grid encourages the viewer to look across the image, viewing the face as a map of experience. However, as the viewer steps back to view the image at a distance, the head reads as a volume drawn with *chiaroscuro*, bright highlights through to the rich deep blacks associated with mezzotint.

There is an extraordinary sense of discipline and commitment in Close's printwork. A fingerprint serves as the indexical mark in *Leslie/Fingerprint*,1986, cross-hatch in *Self-Portrait*, 1977, or the drop of acid on to aquatint as in *Self-Portrait/Spitbite/White on Black*, 1997. As was revealed in the touring exhibition Chuck Close Prints: Process & Collaboration, out of these often simple propositions, startlingly complex and arresting images result.[5]

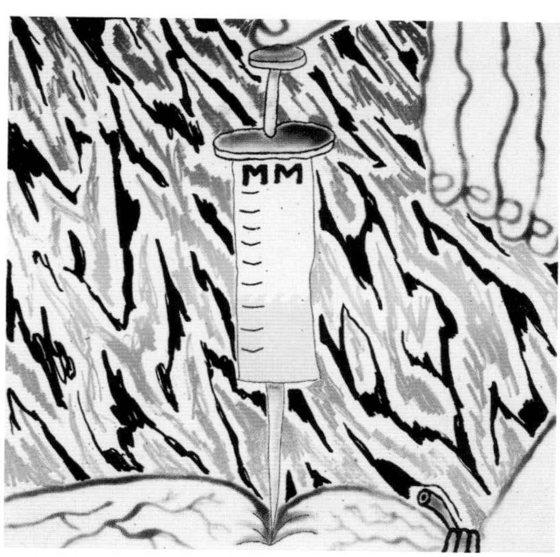

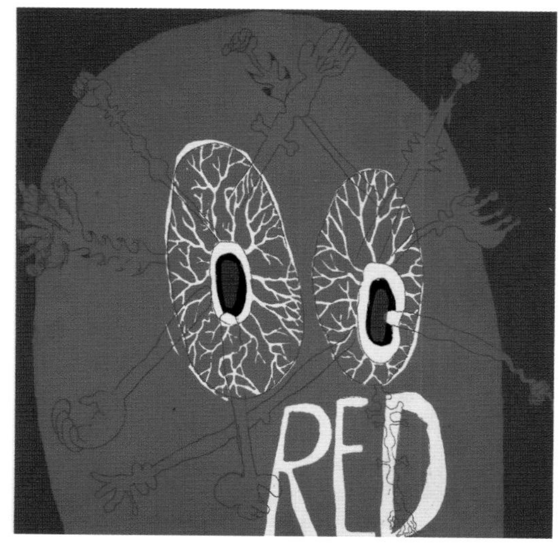

below and opposite: TRENTON DOYLE HANCOCK, *Fix*, 2007.
A portfolio of 20 pages, utilising combinations of etching, lithography and silkscreen, 35.5 x 35.5 cm, edition of 30. Printed by Randy Hemminghaus. Published by the Brodsky Center for Innovative Editions. Image courtesy the artist and the Brodsky Center for Innovative Editions.

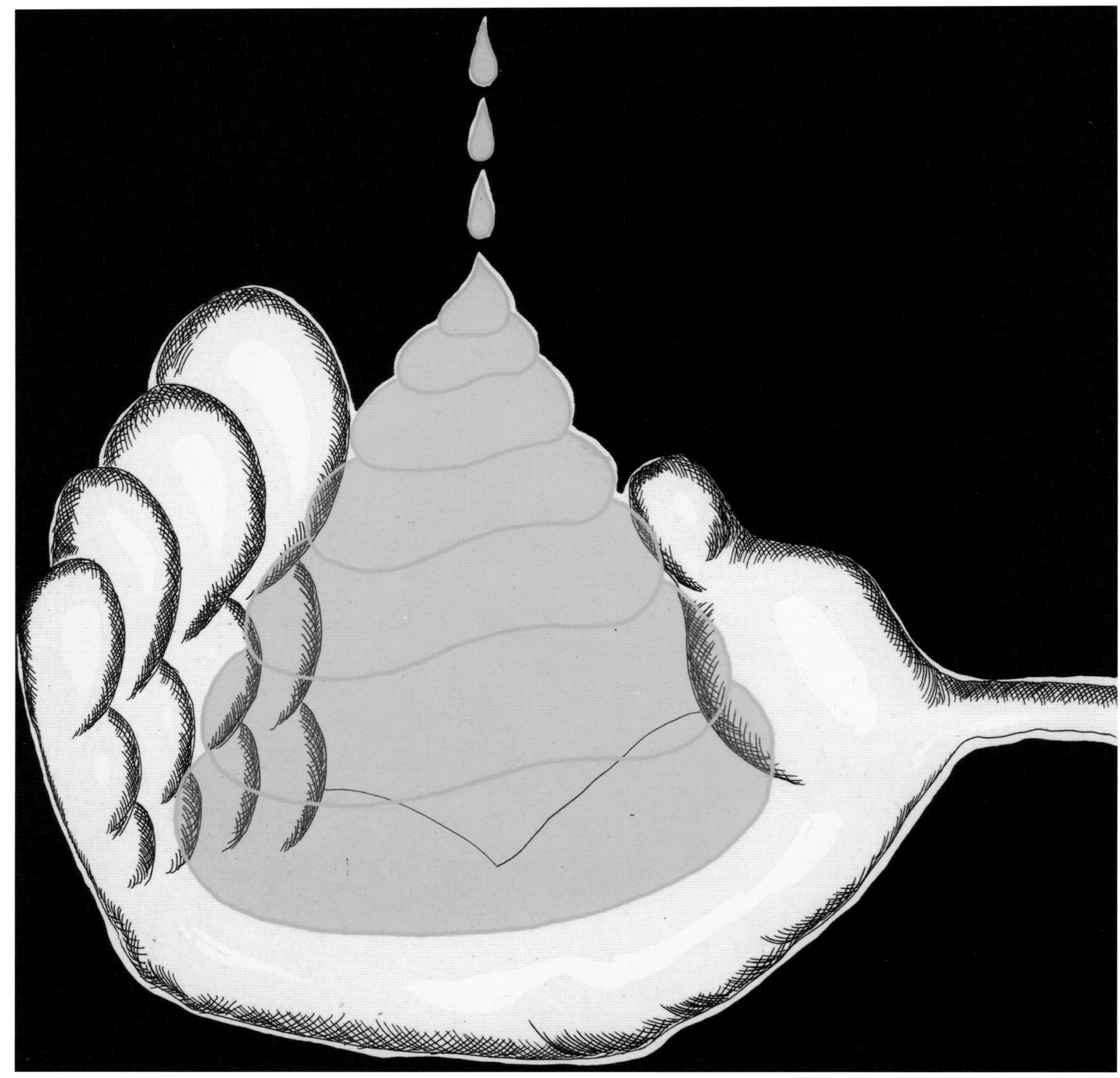

CHUCK CLOSE, *Self-Portrait/Spitbite/ White on Black*, 1997.
Spitbite aquatint, 52 x 40 cm, edition of 50. Photo by Carlin Mayer, courtesy Pace Prints, New York. Image courtesy PaceWildenstein, New York. © Chuck Close.

CHUCK CLOSE, *Keith/Mezzotint*, 1972.
Mezzotint, 129.5 x 105.5 cm, edition of ten. Photo by Maggie L Kundtz, courtesy PaceWildenstein, New York. Image courtesy PaceWildenstein, New York. © Chuck Close.

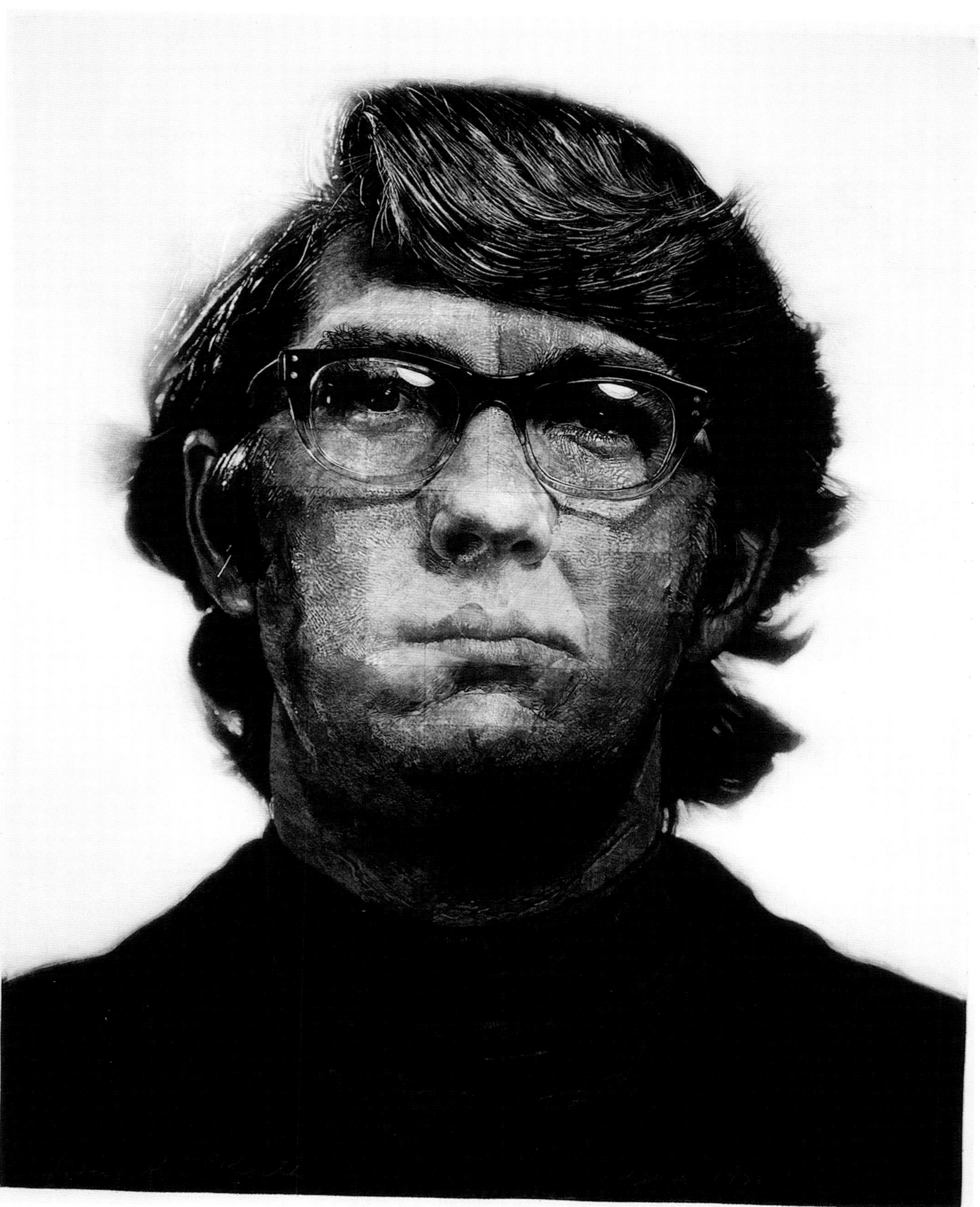

top: STEPHEN CHAMBERS, *The Martyrdom of St Ursula (Giardino)*, 2005.
Monotype, 43.5 x 54.5 cm. Image courtesy Flowers London. © Stephen Chambers.
bottom: STEPHEN CHAMBERS, *Fondamenta*, 2005.
Monotype, 43 x 55 cm. Image courtesy Flowers London. © Stephen Chambers.

While Close tempers his gestures within the structure of the grid, Patrick Caulfield has used the capacity for screenprint to print even, flat areas of saturated colour, removing any evidence of gesture, as the defining characteristic of his remarkable prints. As Mel Gooding writes "... for Caulfield the primary concern has always been to create an impeccable image, a visual proposition lacking the distraction of 'expressive' gesture".[6]

In screenprint, Caulfield immediately found a medium suited to his graphic style of painting. Over a three-year period he produced *Some Poems of Jules Laforgue* a series of 22 screenprints, published in 1973, which act as counterpoints to Laforgue's enigmatic poetry. With the minimum of visual information and a faultless sense of composition, these prints evoke great depths of feeling. His themes of the still life and uninhabited places provide a means for his visual poetry. Again, Gooding writes with rare insight that they "... are evocations of a world in which quiet dramas of happiness and sadness are played out, dates are kept or unkept, conviviality or solitude endured".[7]

While there was complete synchronicity between Caulfield's paintings and prints, both holding the viewer at a similar discreet distance, there is a profound change in scale and feeling between the large-scale paintings and the intimate nature of Peter Doig's prints. The prints, often no larger than 30 x 20 cm are marked by their drawing quality and tentative line. Drawn through soft ground, the line is then developed through etching, in some cases broadening and coarsening the line so it becomes a shape. Printmaking in general imposes flatness on to an image, in particular the intaglio process which stamps down the image under pressure on to the paper. For Doig, this flatness offers an opportunity to intensify that dialogue between the surface and a deeper space. Often working in series, the prints together suggest scenes from a film, repositioning the viewer and compelling them to construct a narrative, which is however, never resolved.

Stephen Chambers and Andrzej Jackowski are both painters that have used print to extend and reflect on their paintings, it being ideally suited to their use of drawing in their work. Their prints can be seen as retaining the spontaneity of sketchbook drawings while endeavouring to fix them as resolved and considered images. Jackowski writes that it was the use of *chine-collé* and the relationship with the printer Simon Marsh at Hope Sufferance Studio that finally enabled him to find a way to work with intaglio... "but it was when he (Simon Marsh) introduced me to *chine-collé* that things took off... suddenly there was texture and colour and more of the feel of my drawings."[8] Jackowski also, interestingly, notes that he works on his prints in phases inbetween batches of paintings but cannot work on prints and paintings at the same time. "They require very different ways of thinking—one (print) is like making jigsaws and thinking things through in advance, the other (painting) is more organic and speculative and takes 12 months!"[9] These prints have the quality of small paintings, but with an economy of colour—the result of a reduced palette.

Stephen Chambers has made a variety of prints, in a variety of media. In collaboration with printers Mike Taylor and Simon Marsh he has also extended this into monoprint finding the speed of the process particularly exhilarating.

> There is no such thing as a slow monoprint. I've made many hundreds of these. They are made on plates of stainless steel and the imagery is painted on to these plates with oil paint. I tried printing ink but found it too sticky to mix colours at the speed I was thinking. The monotypes are always at least a two-plate process; an initial transparent tone with the painted plate printed second. I stand at a high table, draw in the image with a pencil and paint it in. The painting of the image might take 45 minutes or it might take two hours, depending on the complexity. If it takes much longer than that the paint begins to cloy, becoming tacky and risking sticking, and thereby tearing the paper when put through the press. Conversely, if it goes through the press too soon the paint is too loose, wet, and risks squashing and running.[10]

The nature of the process of monoprint throws greater emphasis on the time spent drawing rather than in processing and they are made in intense periods of time, long days working with the printers, resolving perhaps ten images a day. And it is important for the artist not to interrupt this flow, accepting that the results will be variable "It doesn't matter, the editing takes place at the end."[11]

ANDRZEJ JACKOWSKI, *Vigilant Dreamer*, 2005.
Etching, 52 x 56 cm. Image courtesy Purdy Hicks Gallery. © Andrzej Jackowski.

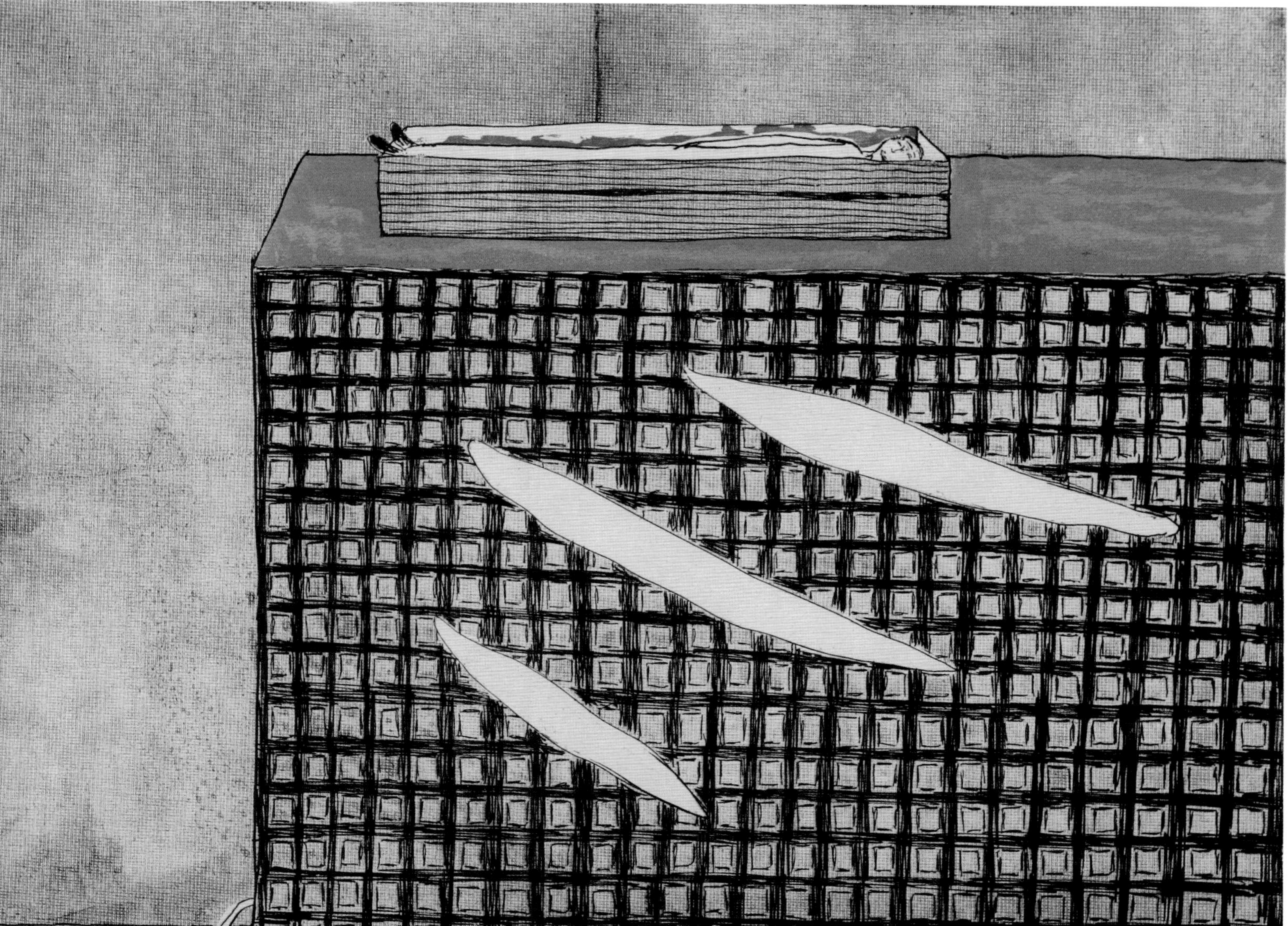

ANDRZEJ JACKOWSKI, *Station*, 2005.
Etching, 51 x 60.5 cm. Image courtesy Purdy Hicks Gallery.

THE HYBR

EDUARDO PAOLOZZI, *Calcium Light Night* from *Four German Songs*, 1974–1976. Screenprint on paper, 69.5 x 51 cm. Courtesy The Eduardo Paolozzi Foundation. © Tate, London 2009.

D PRINT

The print can be the result of a combination of processes and approaches and on to any number of surfaces as well as paper. From Robert Rauschenberg's *Hoarfrost* mixed media prints on layers of cloth (satin, cheese cloth and silk), to Mick Moon's collaged printed surfaces and Joe Tilson's print and collage assemblages, the solutions are wide ranging. Eduardo Paolozzi's screenprints, Anne Desmet's assembled wood engravings, Charlotte Hodes' digital laser-cuts and Peter Blake's and the artists' collective Faile's engagement with popular imagery, also provide evidence of the way collage has been used within printmaking.

Rauschenberg and Paolozzi represent two distinct polarities in their approaches to the collage possibilities through print. Rauschenberg was alive to the physicality of process, signalling his direct approach early in his career when in 1953 he produced with John Cage, *Automobile Tire Print*, a print measuring 42 x 670 cm, of a tyre mark in ink on paper, a sharp riposte to the fetished mark of the New York School. Again in 1963, when the lithographic stone he had drawn, cracked in half during proofing, Rauschenberg turned this to his advantage and went on to edition the print complete with fracture entitled *Accident*, 1936.

> Undeterred, he retained the diagonal white gash through the composition, recording this event. When *Accident* won first prize at the prestigious Ljubljana Graphic Biennial in 1963, it established Rauschenberg, ULAE, and American printmaking in the forefront as never before.[1]

But it was in printmaking through the languages of photography and drawing that he generated some of his most memorable prints. In 1974, working with Gemini G.E.L. he produced the series *Hoarfrost*. These were screenprinted images printed on to separate sheets of thin translucent material, then overlaid to create an image evoking transparency and shifting relationships, causing the critic Robert Hughes to eulogise:

> The latest result includes some of the most remarkable graphic images made by a living artist: Rauschenberg's *Hoarfrost* suite... They are out of the familiar Rauschenberg image bank again, part random and part (one suspects) autobiographical: newspaper fragments, comic cutouts, a Cessna, a balloon, an octopus, buckets, a hand gripping a squeegee, an ostrich egg and so on.
>
> But they are printed on floating veils of silk, chiffon, muslin and taffeta, one positioned over another. One peers into this soft, gauzy space as though looking through ice crystals diffused on a windowpane: hence the collective title *Hoarfrost*.[2]

ROBERT RAUSCHENBERG, Preview from the series *Hoarfrost Editions*, 1974.
Transfer of photolithograph, newspaper and screenprint on fabric and paper bags, 175.5 x 204.5 cm.
Digital image: The Museum of Modern Art, New York/Scala. © Estate of Robert Rauschenberg.
DACS, London/VAGA, New York 2009.

Paolozzi, a sculptor for whom collage provided a method for all aspects of his work, approached screenprint in collaboration with the printer Chris Prater, to create works of great complexity, humour and irreverence. These prints established a new level of engagement with the process, incorporating a dazzling range of imagery. Drawn from comics, advertising, and technical manuals, these remarkable prints seem to encapsulate the world as known—a visual encyclopaedia and a celebration of contemporary life. These prints provided a counterpoint to his sculptures infused with a wonderful sense of play and delighting in the collisions between high and low culture.

For Peter Blake the source material has been popular culture and ephemera, recalling the collages of printed matter from the Victorian era. The fairground, performers and outsiders have provided a rich landscape of imagery, resulting in prints from the touchingly understated miniature wood engravings of dwarfs and fairground entertainers, *Tiny T.N.T. Tantrum*, 1973, through to multicoloured screenprints taking the alphabet as a structure for a series of composite images.

A contemporary of Paolozzi and Blake, and also seen within the Pop movement, Joe Tilson originally trained as a carpenter and brought this knowledge and skill into his work as an artist. Tilson's innovative approach to art was extended into printmaking where his work is characterised by breaking the rules and expanding the parameters of what was permitted as print. These works, particularly from the Pop era, embraced a range of new possibilities, including industrial fabrication with enlarged images of 35 mm slides, through to works which showed a painterly disregard for the preciousness often associated with the limited edition. In the *Mantra* series, 1979, the print reveals its own making, with the stencil used in the making of the print attached to the final editioned print with string, suggesting that this is a momentary interruption in the process of making. In conversation with

JOE TILSON, *Earth Mantra*, 1977.
Soft ground etching and aquatint with stencil plate and string collage, paper and image 106 x 76 cm, edition of 71. Printed at Grafica Uno, Milan. Published by Waddington Graphics, London. Courtesy Joe Tilson and Alan Cristea Gallery, London.

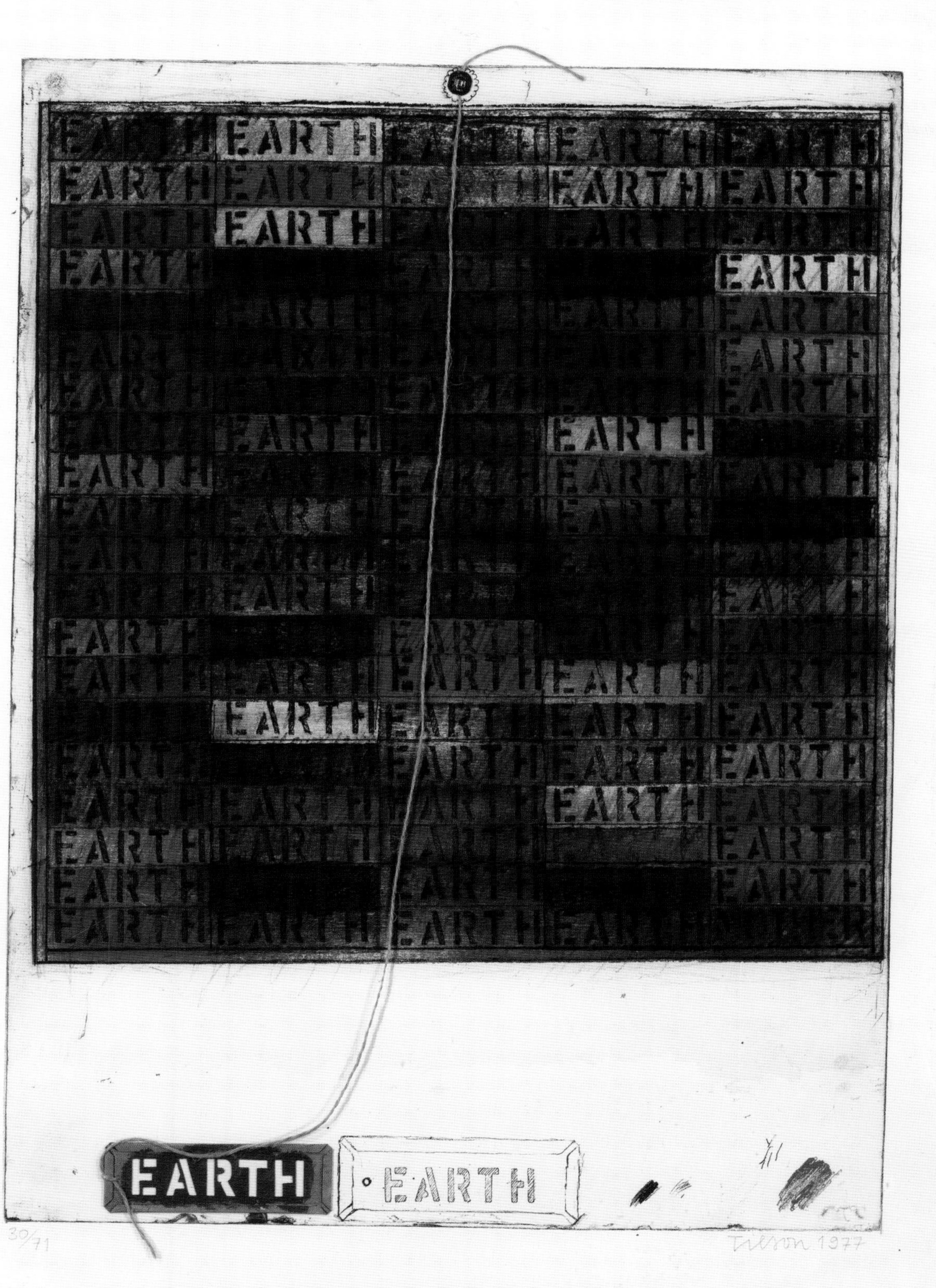

opposite: ANNE DESMET, *Green Glass Light*, 2007.
Wood engraving on paper, collage on to 30 green/gold glass tesserae, 12.2 x 10.5 x 0.5 cm, unique piece. Courtesy the artist.

below: ANNE DESMET, *Babel Flower: dusk*, 2005.
Flexograph printed enlargements from smaller wood engravings, with indented plywood print and glass-headed pins, collage on paper, 79.5 x 79.5 cm, unique edition. Courtesy the artist.

Colin Gleadell, Tilson recalls that "In the 60s, I thought the question, 'What is an original print?' was totally irrelevant. My aim was to make things that corresponded to my feelings and thoughts—not to pre-established categories."[3]

Gleadell goes on to say that Tilson then made a list of things you were not supposed to do in printmaking: "make each print different; paint on prints; tear the paper; crumple and fold the paper; make holes in the print; make three-dimensional prints; glue objects to the print", and so on and then proceeded to do just that.[4]

Whilst Tilson came from a practical artisan training, Tom Phillips, in contrast, has come from a background well-versed in literature, having read English at Oxford (whilst also studying drawing at The Ruskin School of Drawing and Fine of Art) and whose work includes writing, composing, translation and work for opera. In 1966 he began an ongoing project, *A Humument* based on the Victorian novel *A Human Document*. In 1970 a printed version was begun, completed three years later involving screenprint, lithography and letterpress. In both intensity and scale these works echo the illuminated texts of William Blake, operating at that intersection between literature and art.

Anne Desmet brings a variety of processes together in the making of her works, which, whilst referencing architecture, are suggestive of fragments and of fracture. Often using wood engraving, a medium not immediately associated with experimentation, she combines it with a variety of other processes and unexpected media such as glass, mirrors and even razor shells. On a similar intimate scale, but still exploring the very surface of the print Siân Bowen, makes works in which the viewer is left uncertain as to whether her images are coming into being or in the process of fading. In the series *Of Dust*, 2008, she takes photographs of *okoshi-ezu* (eighteenth century Japanese three-dimensional folding teahouse plans) a starting point to explore the relationship between shadow and substance. She describes a bringing together of both contemporary and ancient processes and how the photographs were "silkscreened on to handmade papers which had been meticulously coated with a range of raw and black lacquers, these works also evolved through the age-old Japanese technique of *maki-e*—layers of powdered silver, gold, tin or mica having been dusted across the surfaces and burnished to varying degrees".[5]

SIÂN BOWEN, *Of Dust: No. 9*, 2008.
Silkscreen and Japanese maki-e in powdered gold and black lacquer on handmade gampi paper, 17 x 24 cm. Courtesy the artist.

SIÂN BOWEN, *Of Dust: No. 11*, 2008.
Silkscreen and Japanese maki-e in powdered gold and black lacquer on handmade shibu paper, 19.5 x 27.5 cm. Courtesy the artist.

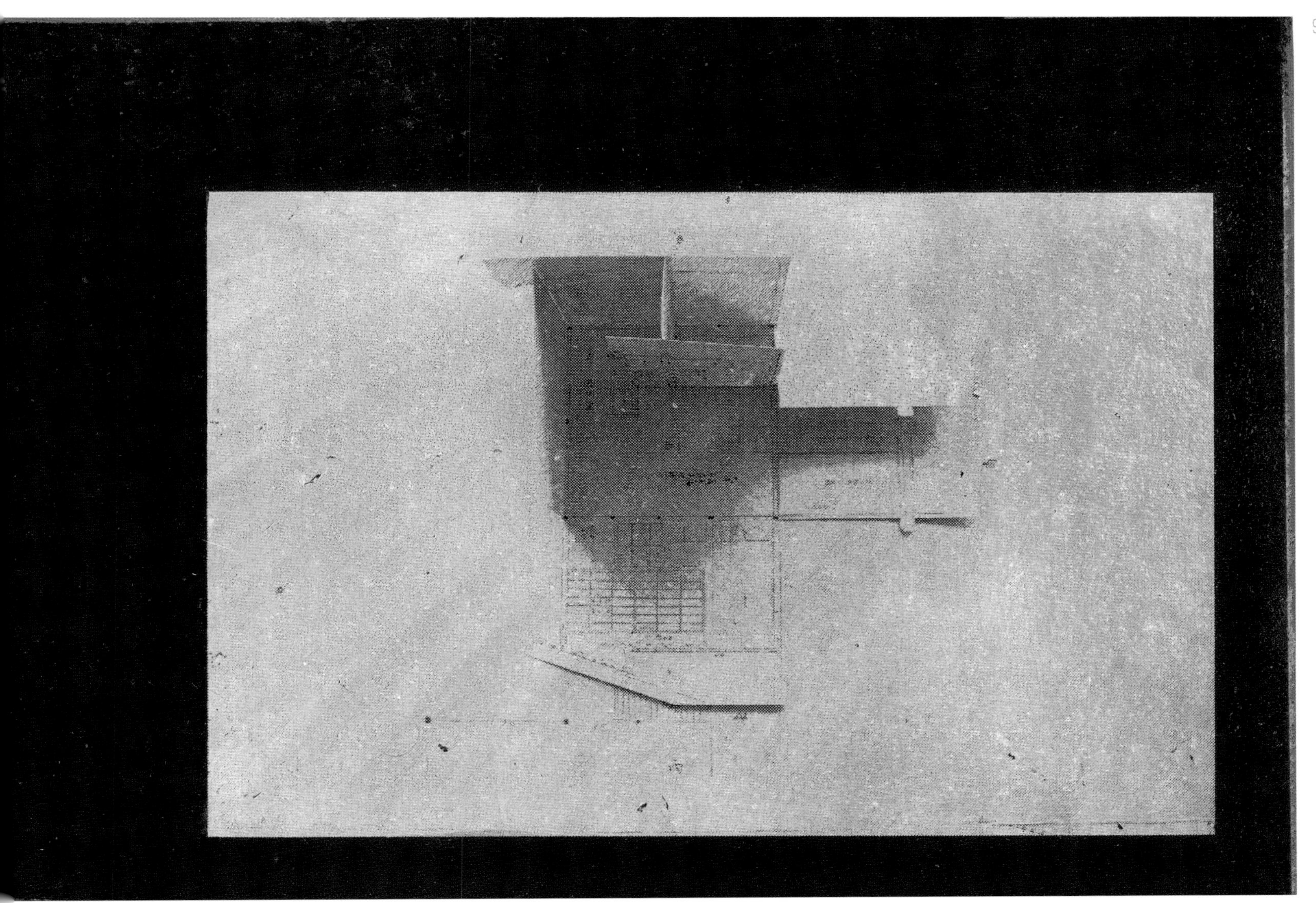

left: CHARLOTTE HODES, *Bather; pink fragments*, 2008.
Laser-cut, 70 x 40 cm. Courtesy Marlborough Fine Art.
right: CHARLOTTE HODES, *Bather; orange glow*, 2008.
Laser-cut, 70 x 40 cm. Courtesy Marlborough Fine Art.

Through treating the whole sheet as the image, she gives them a quality as objects, like old photographs and daguerreotypes, which have been subjected to time, decay and chemical change.

Collage has been at the forefront of Charlotte Hodes' work, a painter who combines a variety of styles and processes from *trompe l'œil* to schematised silhouettes. In a recent set of large-format prints made at the Centre for Fine Print Research, at the University of the West of England, she brings together the lusciousness of the inkjet print with delicate filigree work which is directly laser-cut into the prints themselves. Many of these prints consist of two sheets sandwiched together, enabling her to 'colour' her laser-cut spaces by printing colour on the under sheet. The small fragments of paper—the offcuts of the laser-cutting process—she then collects and uses as collage material pasted on to the surface of the print, producing a further transgression from the accepted norm of the pure printed surface.

Whilst Hodes' freely embraces the possibilities that digital technology now offers, John Utting, a printmaker of long standing, prefers to stick with traditional techniques in the making of his large-format prints. These prints combine woodcut and monoprint and reflect Utting's need for a physical and tactile engagement.

The whole process will usually begin with a flat colour printed from the reverse of the block that carries the cut image.Then a print of the cut image is made on the flat colour, monoprinted additions are made, the qualities of wet on wet ink sometimes incorporated.

The woodblocks are made using a variety of tools, a power drill with various attachments, chisels, sometimes the blocks are sanded back or filled with 'polyfilla' to allow for formal development. Printing is done by hand, applying pressure to the back of the paper with wooden spoons, rollers, etc..[6]

JOHN UTTING, *Fireworks*, 2003–2004.
Woodcut and monoprint, 122 x 91.5 cm. Courtesy the artist.

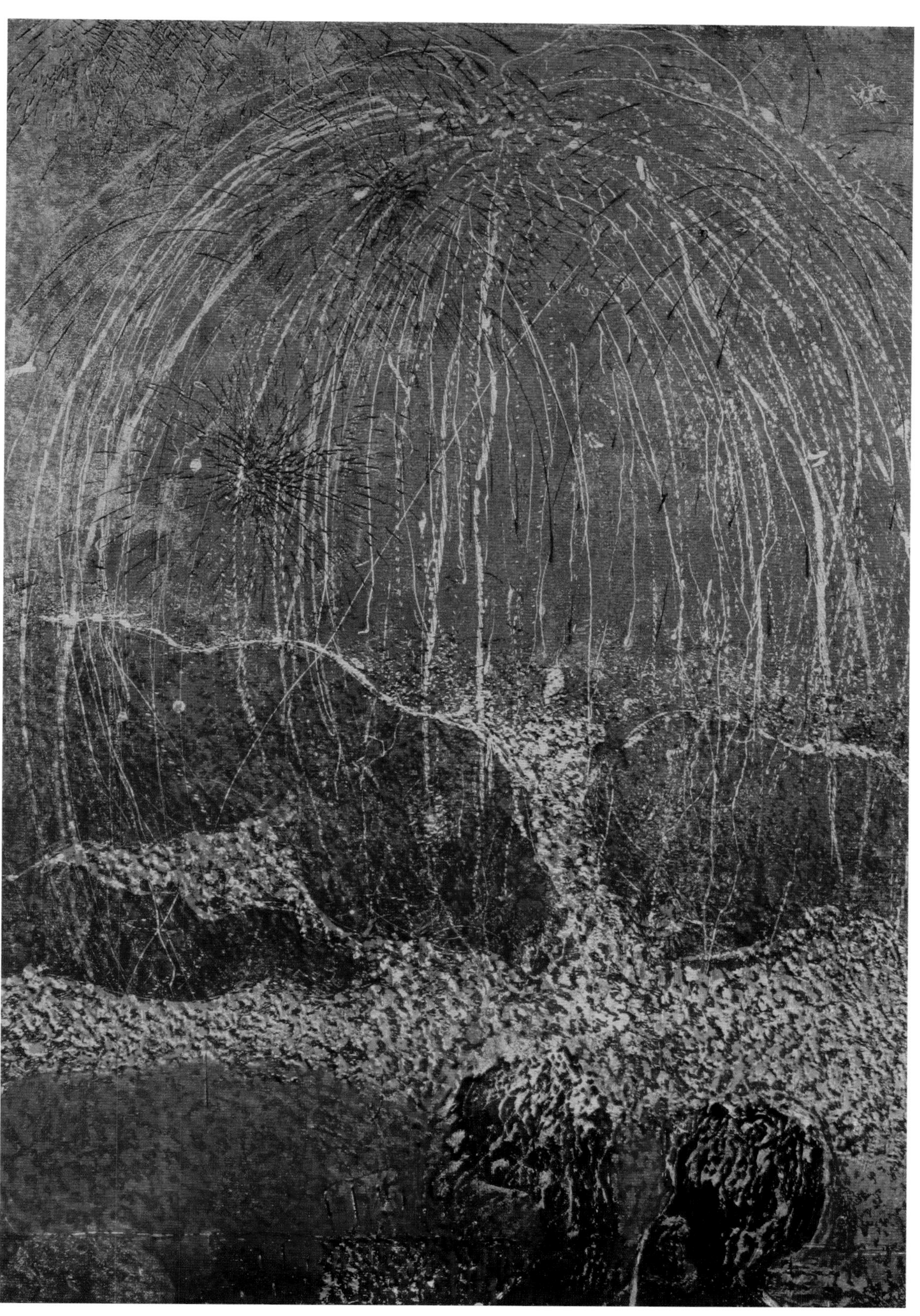

SIGMAR POLKE, *Ohne Titel (Sfumato)*, 1991.
Offset litho, 28 x 25 cm.

HELEN FREDERICK, *Debris*, 2009.
Lithograph, solar plates, digital *chine-collé*, 45.5 x 56 cm. Printed at the University of Tennessee Print Workshop. Courtesy the artist.

The hand-printing, determined by practical necessity, also brings to these works a painterly sensibility, as Utting, eschews the uniformity of a machine printed woodcut for the undulations and variations only possible through the laborious act of hand-printing.

This sensibility is also very apparent in Mick Moon's work, in which monoprinting underpins his practice both in painting and in print, in fact, it becomes almost meaningless to distinguish one from the other.

While unevenness and blemishes are often integral to the handmade approach, Sigmar Polke has paradoxically used offset lithography, the most detached and industrialised of the printing processes, to focus on the very surface qualities and imperfections of the printed images. Much of his work has engaged with the half-tone dot as the process through which photographic images are transfigured as printed material. By enlarging the dot structure, he creates in his images a tension between the image as illusion and the surface as fact. In *Ohne Titel (Sfumato)*, 1991, he presents pairs of photographic images, already degraded through photocopying. While on one side the image is presented complete, on the other is a detail taking a section of the photograph which contains a pronounced flaw, a printing blemish. This image is so enlarged as to become abstract. The viewer then seeks to locate the abstract flaw within the whole photograph and visa versa, suggesting an endless cross-referencing and alternation between figuration and abstraction.

Unlike Peter Blake whose work suggests the passion of the collector, Polke's images feel like fragments, torn from their context, just part of the mountain of printed detritus that pervades everyday life. Helen Frederick, an artist and founder of Pyramid Atlantic, a non-profit contemporary arts centre, takes collage and the fragmented image to make works which range from installation through to artists' books. In two recent works, *Debris*, 2009, and *Monopoly*, 2007, she demonstrates how printing can both be a medium to bring together a range of techniques, reminiscent of Rauschenberg's bricolage approach, as well as itself being a process for the manufacture of collage material.

The artists' collective Faile, formed in 1999, takes the street as the place to be, originally flyposting their images on any available space in New York. Like Polke, they draw heavily on found images, their work, a heady mix of imagery from advertising, cheap handouts, magazines, comics and pornography, create a rich collage that seems to challenge the projection of a coherent society. In Faile, there is a the wild collision of street culture, a world where super heroes do battle with cartoon animals, where Manga meets Marvel comics, all against a backdrop of urban desires. Their practice perfectly illustrates the manner in which printmaking feeds off the plethora of printed material and the residue of urban life to form new works, surprising juxtapositions and challenging propositions.

MICK MOON, *Hybrids*, 1990–1991.
A series of six screenprints with woodblock on Velin Arches 400 gsm paper, paper 137.5 x 109 cm / image 109 x 83.5 cm (each), edition of 45. Printed at Advanced Graphics, London. Published by Waddington Graphics, London. Courtesy Mick Moon and Alan Cristea Gallery, London.

MICK MOON, *Melting Pot*, 1990–1991.
A series of six screenprints with woodblock on Velin Arches 400 gsm paper, paper 137.5 x 109 cm / image 109 x 83.5 cm (each), edition of 45. Printed at Advanced Graphics, London. Published by Waddington Graphics, London. Courtesy Mick Moon and Alan Cristea Gallery, London.

MICK MOON, *Blue Blend*, 1990–1991.
A series of six screenprints with woodblock on Velin Arches 400 gsm paper, paper 137.5 x 109 cm / image 109 x 83.5 cm (each), edition of 45. Printed at Advanced Graphics, London. Published by Waddington Graphics, London. Courtesy Mick Moon and Alan Cristea Gallery, London.

MICK MOON, *Green Spice*, 1990–1991.
A series of six screenprints with woodblock on Velin Arches 400 gsm paper, paper 137.5 x 109 cm / image 109 x 83.5 cm (each), edition of 45. Printed at Advanced Graphics, London. Published by Waddington Graphics, London. Courtesy Mick Moon and Alan Cristea Gallery, London.

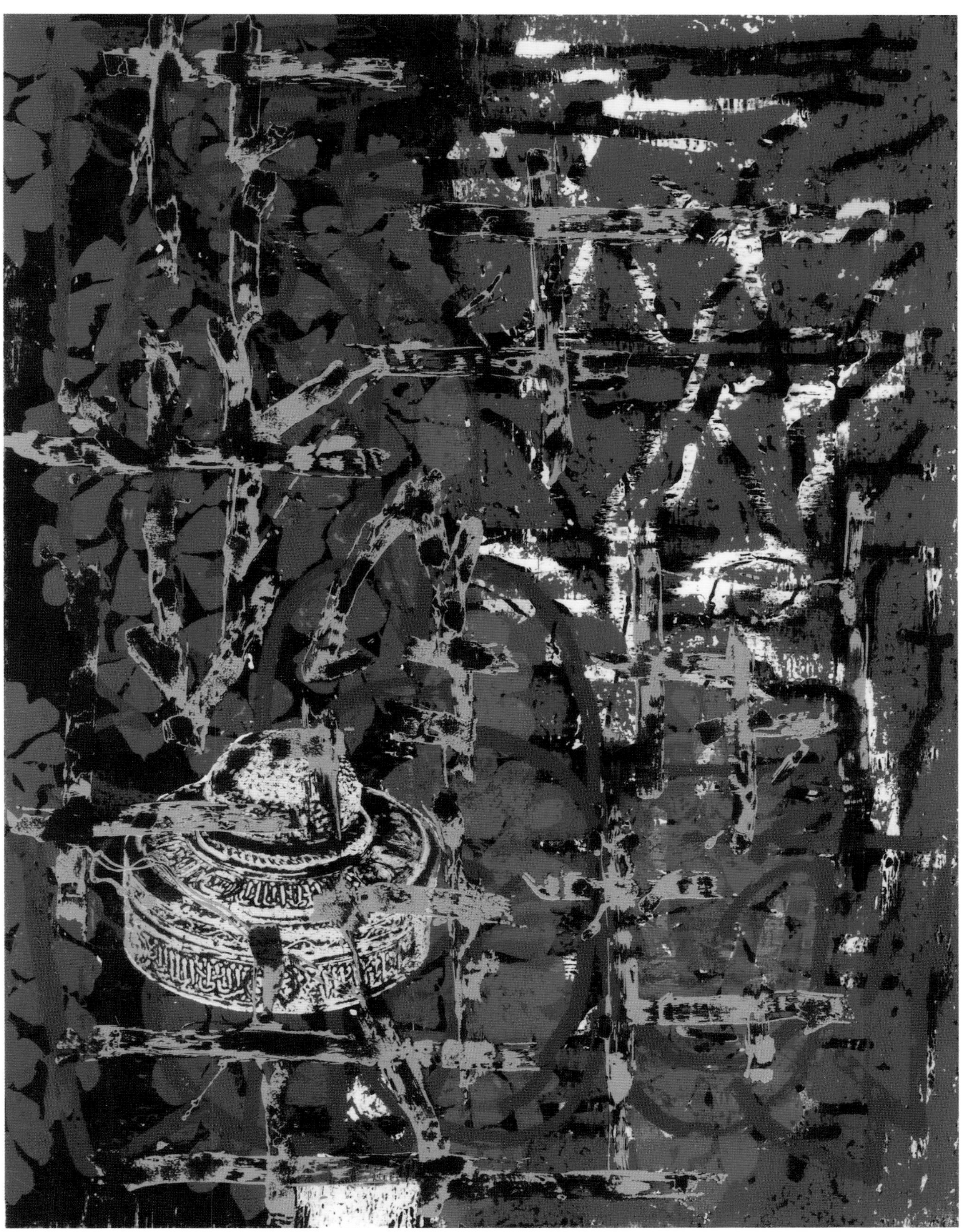

FAILE COLLECTIVE, *My Confessions Stencil*, 2008.
Intaglio-wiped wood print, acrylic and spraypaint, Somerset Textured 300 gsm, 75 x 104 cm, edition of 11. Courtesy the artists.

FAILE COLLECTIVE, *Sexy Ads Pink*, 2008.
Acrylic and silkscreen ink, lenox 100 paper, 63.5 x 96.5 cm. Unique Variant. Courtesy the artists.

PO
IMPER

LITICAL ATIVES

BARTOLOMEU DOS SANTOS, *Entrance to a Labyrinth*, 1976.
Etching and aquatint, 42.5 x 43 cm. Courtesy the Bartolomeu dos Santos Estate.

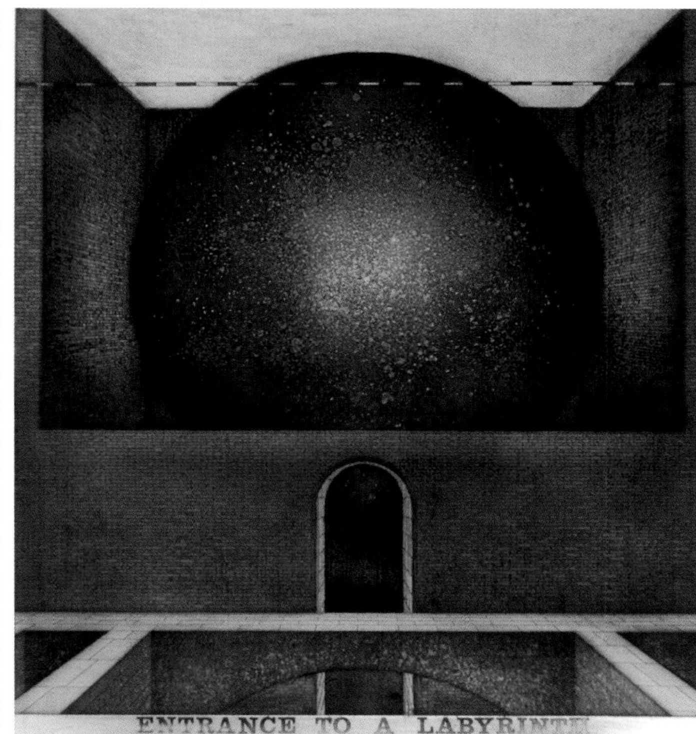

A strong tradition within printmaking has been to evoke change through the distribution of the multiple image. The fact that no single individual can own the work outright contributes to it reaching a very wide audience, with prints being circulated with relative ease. In this Chapter some of the ways print has been used to register resistance or be a vehicle for change will be considered, from Bartolomeu dos Santos' etchings, which challenged the political repression in Portugal, to Kara Walker and Willie Cole in their use of print to confront racial history and to Peter Kennard's and Cat Picton Phillipps' use of the medium as a direct political tool of protest against war and nuclear proliferation.

Printmaking has historically been an ideal medium to critique political and social issues. There is an immediacy and urgency within print that lends itself to an engagement with movements for change. The printed image becomes synonymous with the pamphlet and the newspaper as a means to disseminate propaganda or simply ideas outside of the mainstream to a wider public.

Honoré Daumier's staggering output of daily images for various publications throughout nineteenth century France provided a critical source of opposition to the establishment, while Charles Philipon was imprisoned for his biting satirical print, *The Metamorphosis of King Louis-Philippe into a Pear*, 1831. William Hogarth meanwhile reflected on the sickness below the surface of English respectability, while Francisco Goya and Otto Dix respectively produced etchings graphically depicting the overwhelming tragedy and intense suffering of war. Prints have a way of getting through, they are easily transportable and like poems can be passed around, and used to exert pressure for change.

Bartolomeu dos Santos, a Portuguese artist, adopted a surreal approach to challenge authoritarian regimes. In his etchings and aquatints, Bishops huddle in a ship, floating adrift in a sea of ghostly jelly fish, as in *Portuguese men of war*, 1961, a metaphor for Portugal under dictatorship. More recently in protest against American foreign policy, a crowd of demonic 'Mickey Mouses' parody Joe Rosenthal's iconic photograph of *Raising the Flag on Iwo Jima*, 1945. Elsewhere dos Santos' images of labyrinths or city walls evoke a profound sense of disquiet. Etching was his prime means of expression, particularly aquatint, which he used with complete disregard for the niceties associated with the art. Endlessly reworking the plates, cleaning back with power tools and emery paper, dos Santos' approach to printmaking was physical and sometimes brutal, treating the plate as a surface to battle against.

War and conflict are the recurring themes in Peter Kennard's and Cat Picton Phillipps' collaborative work. Kennard who has been at the forefront of politically engaged art for over three decades, now works in partnership with Phillipps. Moving from old technologies of cut and paste montage, through to digital, their work has endeavoured to retain a sense of physical presence and an urgency to engage in contemporary issues. These priorities take precedence over any thought of longevity or indeed the requirements of the art market, as is apparent in the following exchange:

BARTOLOMEU DOS SANTOS, *Portuguese men of war*, 1961.
Aquatint, 43 x 48 cm. Courtesy the Bartolomeu dos Santos Estate.

BARTOLOMEU DOS SANTOS, *Battle*, 1999.
Etching and aquatint watercoloured, 19 x 24.5 cm. Courtesy the Bartolomeu dos Santos Estate.

KENNARDPHILLIPPS, *Control Room*, 2006.
Pigment ink, charcoal, acrylic and paper on newspaper, 270 cm x 500 cm.
Courtesy kennardphillipps.

SANG-GON CHUNG, *Dark Sea—K*, 2004.
Digital print, 150 x 150 cm. Courtesy the artist.

Paul Coldwell: There is also something rather paradoxical about your work. Here you are, now using state-of-the-art machines, which claim that the prints will last for a 100 years and you are printing them on newspaper where the acid from the paper will destroy the image in a matter of weeks!

Peter Kennard: Well, I like working with the cleanliness and precision of the inkjet and then to work against it, against the medium. It's something to fight against. We didn't need to do this when we used traditional processes because they were dirty to start with. So if you want to work in a hands on way then it does involve breaking down what digital printing was originally conceived as.... When I first made digital prints, they were beautifully printed on Hahnemühle archival paper and there was a sense of aestheticising the subject matter and so through going on to cheap paper and newsprint, it suggests the fragility of the situation that we are making work about, so it's about content.[1]

The Korean artist Sang-gon Chung also responds to current events, filtered through newspaper and TV images. These are not only visual starting points for his images, but also for the manner in which the news reports feed our anxieties as he notes, "The sequence of art work, *Dark Sea,* 2004, quotes newspaper articles and photographs published in relation to the environmental issues in Korea, Japan, and China sharing the same ocean and historical, political, and military trainings and relocations."[2]

In this triptych, originally based on an innocuous newspaper photograph of dolphins breaking the waves, Chung instills a brooding sense of unease. Working digitally, pixel by pixel, the evidence of the dolphins is removed leaving an unsettling view that hovers between figuration and abstraction.

BARBARA KRUGER, *"Untitled" (I shop therefore I am)*, 1987.
Photographic silkscreen/vinyl, 282 x 287 cm. Image courtesy Mary Boone Gallery, New York.

> The image of an abstract sea is created from a detailed image. The vague digitally printed image with collapsed boundaries has two meanings. One is to erase the source of the original copy. This creates a blank and abstract object.... The second meaning is a vague expression as an artist about the bleak future because of subtle and selfish acts taking place in the sea.[3]

In other works, such as *Dark Sea—K*, 2004 the original newspaper photograph of a submarine is once again manipulated and eradicated, hiding the vessel in the process and heightening the sense of menace.

The printed image in the form of advertisements provides the context for Barbara Kruger, 1987, in her efforts to subvert the constant stream of messages aimed at conditioning behaviour. Kruger has produced beautiful prints, which dramatically combine image and text exploring issues of feminism, consumerism and power. Originally trained as a photographer, the work references the cut and paste graphics of magazines combined with the graphic immediacy of Russian posters. The images are memorably direct, her iconic *I shop therefore I am*, 1987, combines in her signature style, clear highlighted text against a red background on top of a coarse photographic image of hands. Measuring almost 300 cm square this screenprint openly competes with the plethora of advertising material that surrounds us.

Wang Guangyi also references the print tradition of the poster, in his case the Chinese revolutionary posters from the Cultural Revolution. In Wang's prints, heroic workers are juxtaposed with Western brands, Coca Cola, Gillette, Chanel, etc., presented with the optimism of a new ideology, suggesting that the move towards capitalism is as profound a change as the Cultural Revolution—Mao's 'Little Red Book' becomes a motif to sell Chanel perfume.

This imperative to engage with a society in flux is apparent in the work of Willie Cole and Kara Walker. Both reference the struggle for racial equality

WILLIE COLE, *Stowage*, 1997.
Woodblock on kozo-shi paper, paper 142 x 264 cm / image 125.5 x 241 cm, edition of 16.
Printed by Derrière L'Etoile Studios. Published by Alexander and Bonin Publishing, New York.
Courtesy of Alexander and Bonin, New York.

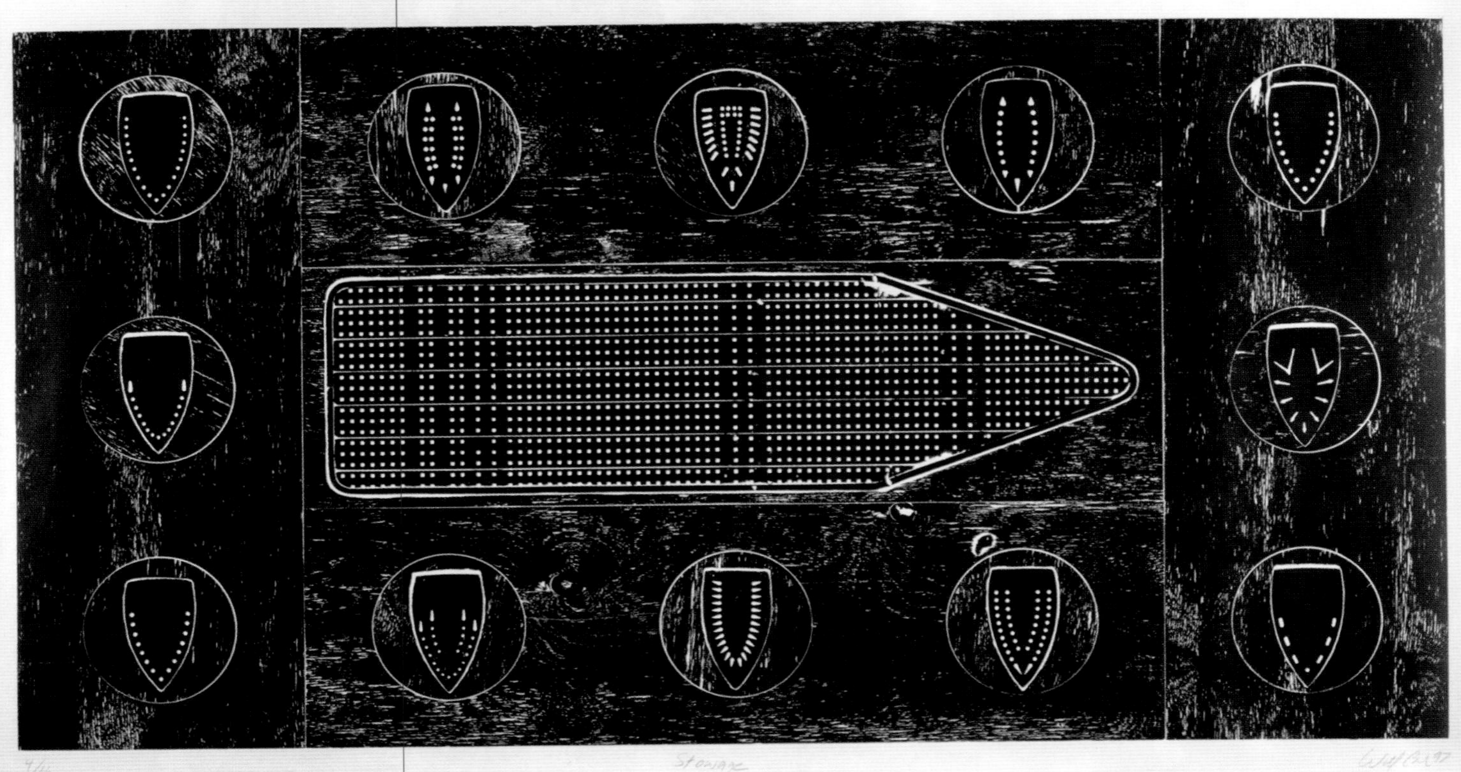

and the manner in which these issues can be fixed in history. Seeking to challenge these readings, Willie Cole has extensively used the iron, with its connotations of domestic work and its similarity to African masks as a recurring motif. It also functions as a graphic reference, sometimes oblique, sometimes implicit, to the floor plans of the slave ships like the *Brookes*, prints of which were extensively used and widely circulated in the campaign against slavery.

In *Stowage*, 1997, Cole takes the floor plan and surrounds it with heraldic images printed directly from the base of irons in a wonderful reworking of this historical print. The woodcut itself, uses the iron's scorch mark as a printing device with all its connotations of branding and violence, with the printed grain of the wood referencing the wooden timbers on to which the slaves would sleep, making an image which both addresses the viewer conceptually as well as physically. His printmaking output also encompasses digitally printed photographic works, most notably a disarmingly elegant series of iris prints, each featuring an iron seen from above in isolation like a tribal mask. Each print is titled from the manufacturers' slogan such as *Loyal and Dependable, Ahead of its Time, Satisfaction Guaranteed,* creating a disquieting reference to the manner in which slaves were advertised and sold.

A similar history permeates Kara Walker's prints, taking images from old publications of the American Civil War, she adds figure silhouettes, unsettling the topographical rendering of the events and taking the image into areas that are more personal and raw. The black silhouettes contrast against the underlying soft lithographic drawing, like shadows in front of a projection implying two conflicting realities.

> Even when the work is celebratory I still hope it has subversion to it, in that all the protagonists are women. That it is we who are the activators. That is not the usual way of the world, but it's symbolic of the way the world could be.[4]

KARA WALKER, *Scene of McPherson's Death. Harper's Pictorial History of the Civil War (Annotated)*, 2005.
Offset lithography and silkscreen, 134.5 x 99 cm. Courtesy the artist and Sikkema Jenkins & Co.

Printmaking is a natural extension of Nancy Spero's practice, predicated as it is within drawing and collage. The works retain the informality of their making, charged with a compulsion and desire to get images out into the world in order to effect change. Images are hand-printed on to paper or stamped directly on to walls. Her working method is to translate images into outline drawings on zinc or rubber plates, which can then be used to print directly on to the walls of her installations or on to paper scrolls. She has assembled an 'alphabet of hieroglyphics' numbering over 500, comprising images taken from magazines, newspapers and art books, from which she draws upon to form a personal vocabulary. This connects printmaking with its most basic manifestation, the printing block or the rubber stamp—tools for multiple printing and infinite variation.

Getting images out of the gallery and into the world could serve as a mantra for the artist known as Banksy whose stencilled additions to public spaces have given him both notoriety and an international reputation. An industry has developed around these images and like Warhol, the difference between mere reproduction and the fine art print becomes a matter for debate. As with his interventions on the street, Banksy uses stencils in his printmaking, not sprayed through, but screenprinted, each colour the result of a separate stencil. Curiously, despite the radical nature of Bansky's practice, these works readily accept the conventions of the limited edition print, printed on handmade paper with publisher's stamp, signed and numbered.

There has been a strong tradition within printmaking of storytelling and narrative, connecting with popular culture and folklore, fantasy and the grotesque. Through this, printmaking has often spoken to and for an underclass, a tool either of specific protest or to assert the imagination over oppression. William Kentridge has consistently made work, in the form of drawings, prints or animations, which reflect on the moral chaos of apartheid.

BANKSY, *Morons*, 2007.
Screenprint, 50 x 70 cm, edition of 150. Image courtesy Pest Control Office.

> I haven't been successful in escaping from Johannesburg. The four houses that I have lived in, my school, my studio, have all been less than two miles from each other. And in the end, all my work is rooted in this rather desperate provincial city. I have never tried to make illustrations of apartheid, but the drawings and films are certainly spawned by and feed off the brutalised society left in its wake. I am interested in a political art, that is to say an art of ambiguity, contradiction, uncompleted gestures and uncertain endings. An art (and a politics) in which optimism is kept in check and nihilism at bay.[5]

In the series of intaglio prints, *Ubu tells the truth*, 1996, he reinterprets Alfred Jarry's play *Ubu Roi*, showing the character of Ubu as a split personality, divided between public and private as if in a continuous state of torment. Drawing is central to Kentridge's work, which not only informs and shapes his prints but has provided a means through which he has developed an important body of animated films, painstakingly built up from drawings, recorded as they develop and change, through erasure and additions.

The grotesque is also the context for Victor Manuel Hernandez Castillo, an artist from Mexico whose large linocuts describe a claustrophobic vision of tortured souls where humans and animals struggle to survive. There is a sense of society at the edge of chaos as Castillo notes,

> My graphic creations have a metaphoric meaning, thus in my opinion, it is very important to the observer to make his/her own interpretation and own narrative. In some cases these might become anecdote... where humans share their beings with animals, creating hybrid forms.[6]

While it is clear that some artists like Kennard and Phillipps and Kruger have adopted clear strategies in their use of print in order to disseminate and create change, equally there are others who are drawn to the medium as a means of engaging with their imaginations, as with Kentridge and Castillo. For both approaches, printmakers offer a direct contact with a broad and diverse public, without the preciousness associated with high art, and through this they are able to infiltrate and be active in bringing about change.

WILLIAM KENTRIDGE, *L' Inesorabile Avanzata: Massacre of the Innocents*, 2007.
Sugar-lift aquatint, drypoint and engraving, paper 40 x 35 cm / image 20 x 15 cm, edition of 50.
Image courtesy David Krut Print Worshop. © William Kentridge.

THE SCU

LOUISE BOURGEOIS, *Do Not Abandon Me*, 2000.
Drypoint on paper, 49 x 40.5 cm. Photo by Christopher Burke. Courtesy Harlan & Weaver, New York.

LPTOR'S PRINT

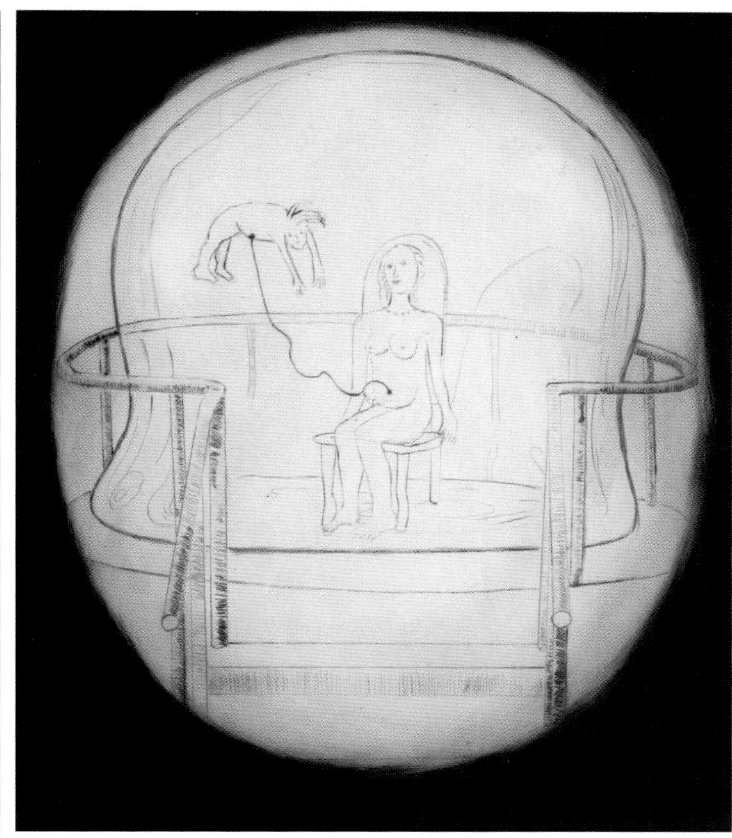

Printmaking has often served sculptors in a very different way to that of painters. Whilst it is obvious that, for painters, the translation from paint to print often requires a rethinking of scale and negotiating process, for the sculptor, the translation of ideas from three-dimensional to two-dimensional can produce images that open up a fresh interpretation of the artist's intention. In some cases it can result in bodies of work, which stand distinct in their own right as it is for Louise Bourgeois, for whom printmaking has been a vital aspect of her practice over decades.

Bourgeois worked at Stanley William Hayter's Atelier 17 in New York in the 1940s, where she produced the enigmatic series of prints entitled *He Disappeared into Complete Silence*, 1947 which brought together etchings with drypoints with her own text relating a story of jealousy, violence and surreal humour. The prints reference the New York tenement blocks, suggesting interior and exterior spaces and an overriding sense of isolation and the ensuing difficulty of communication.

> The images present a microcosm of absurdity. Architectonic forms—buildings or the artist's easel—acquire both totemic and human characteristics, unsettlingly claustrophobic interiors defeat the promise of escape offered by the ladders, bleakly transparent look-out towers contain fires to ward off the evil spirits of depression, and mechanistic personages spar with each other.[1]

All of her intaglio prints retain and heighten the sense of touch, not as a fetishised mark or gesture, but as the direct manifestation of hand and eye. In *Do Not Abandon Me*, 2000, the delicate drypoint evokes the fragility and vulnerability of the mother and child, the child floating like a balloon still attached by the umbilical cord. Another sculptor, for whom drypoint serves as a graphic tool, is Ana Maria Pacheco, a Brazilian artist whose monumental carved painted tableaux bring together religious iconography with that of political abuse and torture. Drypoint becomes the equivalent to the physical act of carving, while also providing the opportunity for her to dramatically control light and shadow, the deeply incised lines creating dense areas of darkness as the black ink literally bleeds out of the line. Her prints, which vary greatly in terms of scale, can also be seen as mementos or souvenirs of the installations, reminiscent of the early engravings that were sold at religious festivals and saint's day in the Middle Ages. If Pacheco draws on a Catholic tradition, John Davies, in his more recent work, points to a more Eastern influence. His sculptures have predominantly focused on the figure or the head, and often incorporate drawn elements across and on to the surface. In his prints, etchings and aquatints, he develops the ideas from both his sculptures and drawings by making more apparent the sense of ceremony through their glowing pastel colour. The prints also allow the figure to be contained, the surrounding colour

LOUISE BOURGEOIS, *He Disappeared into Complete Silence* (Plate 8), 1947.
Suite of nine engravings with text inside linen covered bookcase, each: 25.5 x 35.5 cm.
Photo by Christopher Burke. Courtesy Cheim & Read, Galerie Karsten Greve and Galerie Hauser & Wirth.

Plate 8

Once an American man who had been in the army for three years became sick in one ear.

His middle ear became almost hard.

Through the bone of the skull back of the said ear a passage was bored.

From then on he heard the voice of his friend twice, first in a high pitch and then in a low pitch.

Later on the middle ear grew completely hard and he became cut off from part of the world.

ANA MARIA PACHECO, *Dark Event*, 2007.
Plates I, II, IV and V from a series of seven drypoints, with colour on Plate IV printed *à la poupée* with hand finishing, 68 x 60.5 cm. Published by Pratt Contemporary Art 2007. Courtesy Pratt Contemporary Art.

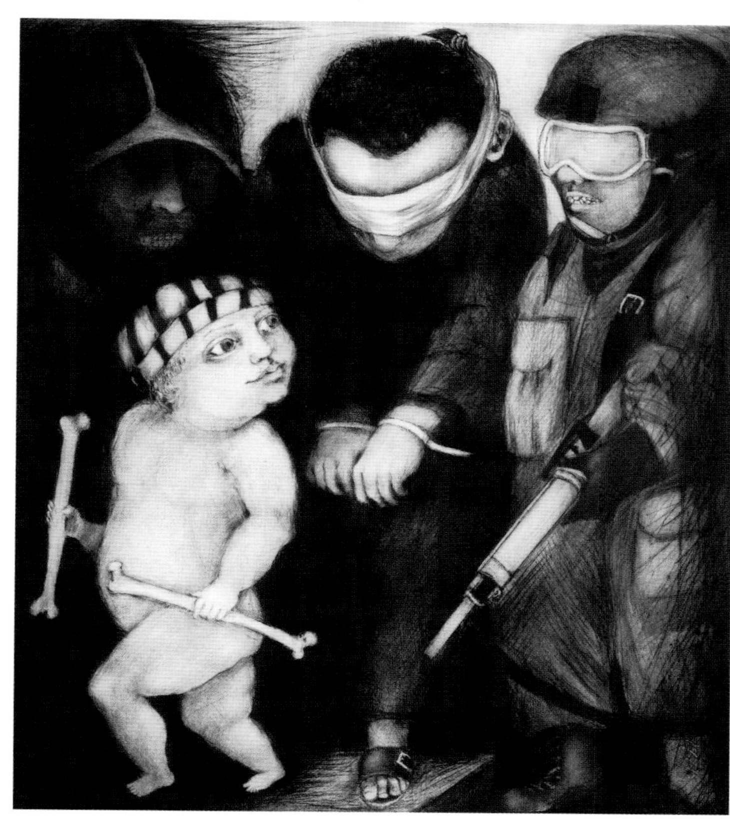

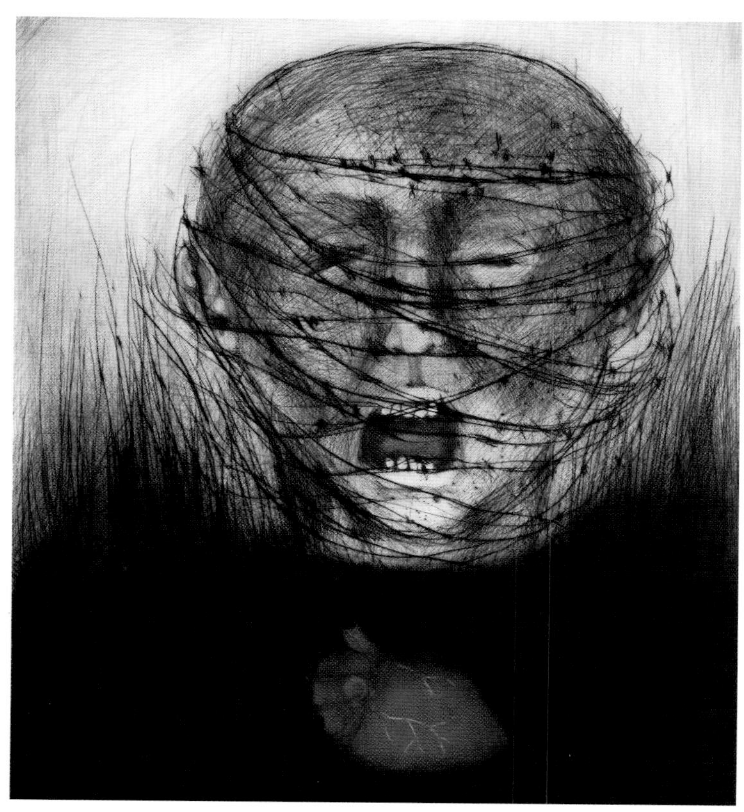

JOHN DAVIES, *Tama for a Man*, 2002.
Etching and aquatint, paper 49 x 36 cm / plate 25 x 15 cm, edition of 20.
Courtesy of Marlborough Fine Art (London) Ltd. © John Davies.

JOHN DAVIES, *Tama for a Woman*, 2002.
Etching and aquatint, paper 49 x 36 cm / plate 25 x 15 cm, edition of 20.
Courtesy of Marlborough Fine Art (London) Ltd. © John Davies.

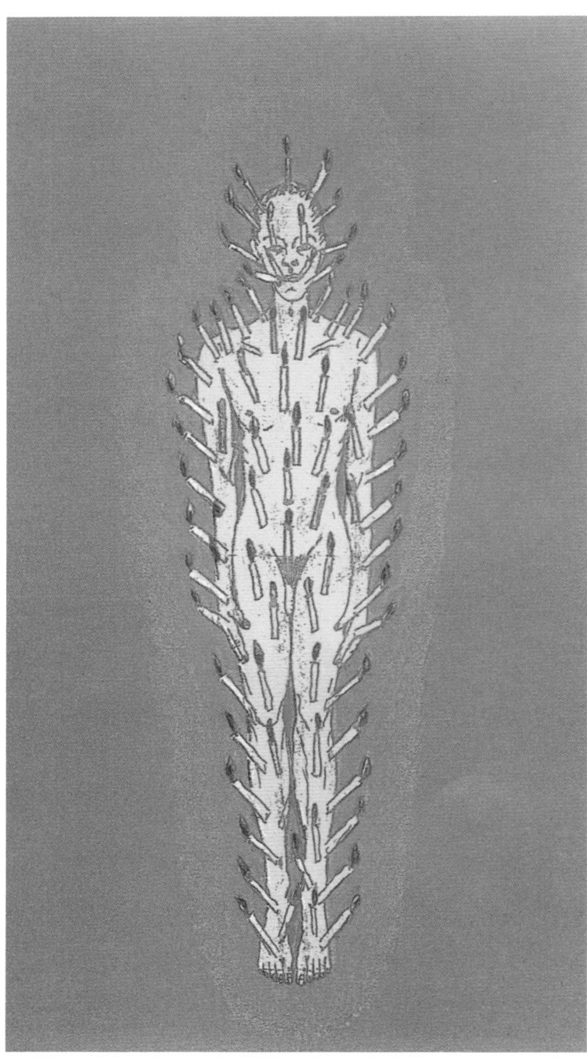

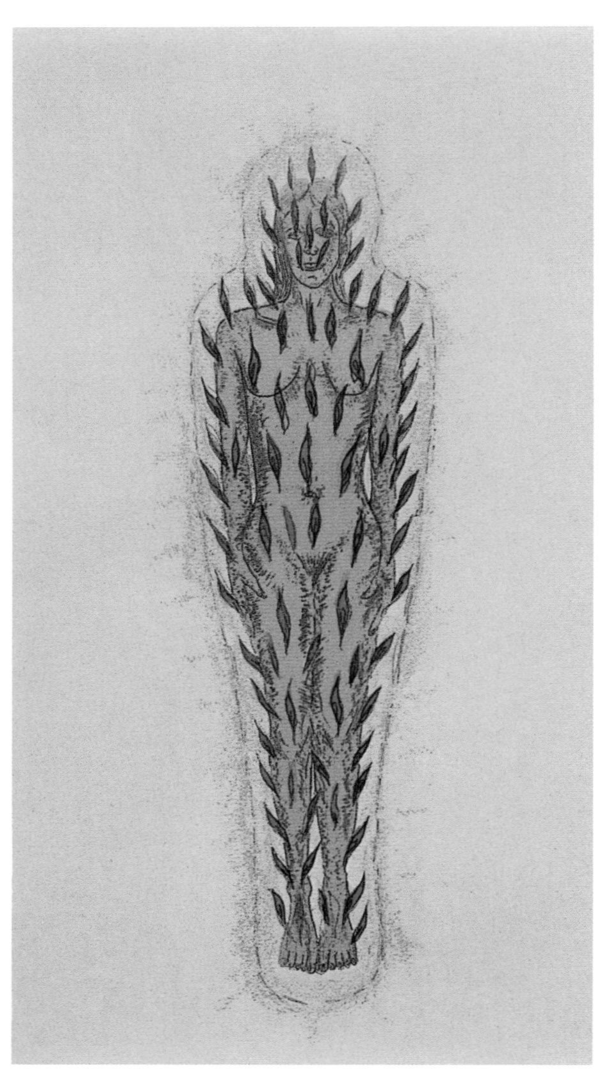

determining an emotionally charged environment in which to view the figure. The colour in these prints is more celebratory in contrast to the sculptures that have been characterised by a more subdued naturalism.

Kiki Smith brings her sculptural concerns with paper and fragility directly into her print works. The prints themselves reflect the same sensibility to materials as her sculptures and installations, the paper being an active element in the development of the image as opposed to merely being a support. In her prints, Japanese paper with its organic and individual character is not only the support for the image but becomes an active poetic element in her exploration of sexuality and vulnerability. The motif of the solitary female figure is explored through a variety of media and formats, from the etching *Sueño*, 1992, where the figure is drawn from the inside out, floating on a single sheet of Japanese paper, to *Free Fall*, 1994, printed on a large piece of paper, folded as if a map. This use of paper as an intrinsic ingredient in her prints is further seen in the majestic *Peacock*, 1997, covering almost four square metres and printed on ten sheets of thin Japanese paper, and in the large-format *Untitled (Negative Legs)*, 1991, featuring 30 sets of legs arranged in a grid, the legs dissolving into pattern.

Tony Cragg, the British sculptor whose work, more than any other of his generation, opened up a radical use of materials, from plastic flotsam arranged as mosaics to sand blasted glass bottles stacked on shelves, has worked within more conventional parameters when making prints.

They reveal the importance of the role of drawing as a thinking process in his work and demonstrate how this serves to inform his sculptures. In fact, the act of drawing is often an integral part of many of his sculptures, with Cragg literally drawing on to them as in *Village*, 1988, or as in *Under the Skin*, 1994, where he uses hundreds of picture hooks screwed into the surface of the sculpture to act as graphic marks to interrupt a direct reading of the forms. In the series of prints *Laboratory Still Lifes*, 1988, he references back to his early training as a scientist, using the landscape of beakers, funnels, glass bottles and flasks as source material. The prints, made at Crown Point Press, are exquisite in their use of spitbite etching, using the acid itself to slowly draw the objects into being. Cragg focuses on the very essence of etching, the action of acid on metal, making explicit the relationship between the image and process and the role of experiment in both art and science.

KIKI SMITH, *Peacock*, 1997.
Etching, ink on Nepal paper, 181.5 x 194 cm. Digital image: The Museum of Modern Art, New York/Scala, Florence. Courtesy PaceWildenstein, New York. © Kiki Smith.

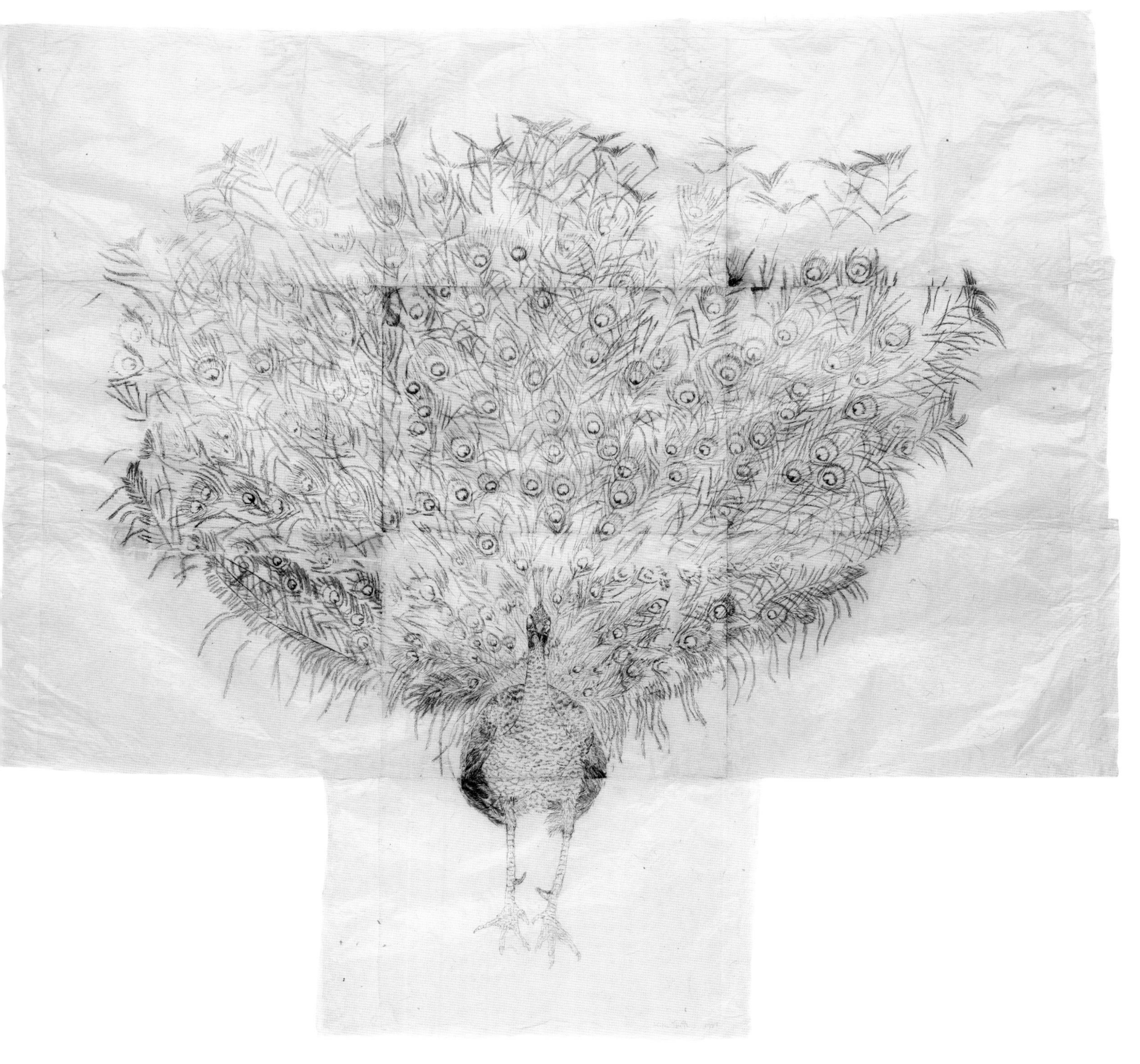

top: TONY CRAGG, *Laboratory Still Life No.2*, 1988.
Aquatint and spitbite on paper. 29 x 90.5 cm. © Tony Cragg.

bottom left: TONY CRAGG, *Laboratory Still Life No.1*, 1988.
Aquatint and spitbite on paper. 30 x 35 cm. © Tony Cragg.
bottom right: TONY CRAGG, *Laboratory Still Life No.3*, 1988.
Aquatint and spitbite on paper. 30 x 35 cm. © Tony Cragg.

TONY CRAGG, *Laboratory Still Life No.4*, 1988.
Aquatint with spitbite and soap ground aquatints and flat bite etching, 46 x 48.5 cm.

RACHEL WHITEREAD, *Cup & Saucer*, 2008.
Cup and saucer moulded from dolls house china and then cast in silicon bronze, hand-painted and with gold leaf rim. Presented in a handmade Douglas-fir presentation box with an etched satin stainless steel plate incorporating description, numbering and signature, cup diameter 8 x depth 6.5 cm / saucer diameter 14 x depth 2 cm / box 17 x 23 x 33 cm, edition of 25. Casting and hand-painting by AB Fine Art Foundry Ltd., London. Boxes made by Woodbourne (Furniture) Limited, London. Published by Alan Cristea Gallery, London. Courtesy Rachel Whiteread and Alan Cristea Gallery, London

Paragon Press, who have been innovative in a publishing programme which has focused on the artists' portfolio, have been responsible for encouraging a number of British sculptors to work their ideas through printmaking; three particular examples being, Richard Deacon, Rachel Whiteread and Bill Woodrow. It is a testament to the freedom offered to the artist through this imprint, that not only are the results so strikingly different in approach and realisation, but that the resulting folios can be seen as iconic works in the artists' overall *œuvre*.

In 1996, Deacon, produced a memorable set of 12 large-format screenprints in greys and blacks, *Show and Tell*, which juxtaposed photographs from the artist's archive with inset drawings. Whilst never directly illustrative, the drawings reference elements from the photographs, offering a rare insight into the source of Deacon's abstract language. The photographs are not in themselves dramatic, a flock of birds flying, detail of a bees' nest, a Romanesque carving, but through the addition of the drawings the viewer is compelled to explore the photograph, retracing the sculptor's thoughts and engaging the viewer in the very act of looking.

Rachel Whiteread is known for her casts of voids, the space under chairs, the air in a room and, most famously, the interior space of a terraced house in East London. In *Demolished*, 1996, in three sequences of four prints, she records the demolition of three high-rise estates in London in screenprinted photographic prints in silvery greys. The prints become equivalents of her sculptural practice set within a tradition of minimalism and formal priorities, the monochrome of her plaster casts matched by the black and white photographs. There is also perhaps a comment on the fact that *House*, 2004, her work that drew worldwide attention, was itself demolished in spite of its critical success. She has more recently worked with digital technology; using laser-cutting to make *Herringbone Floor*, 2009, a delicate lattice cut in thin birch-ply of the spaces inbetween parquet blocks of flooring and in *Secondhand*, 2004, in which she uses stereolithography, a process of printing an object, layer by layer from information derived from scans, to make a three-dimensional print based on dolls' house furniture.

BILL WOODROW, *Ar from The Periodic Table*, 1994.
Linocut, 50 x 43 cm. Published by Charles Booth-Clibbon and The Paragon Press, London.
Image courtesy The Paragon Press, London. © Bill Woodrow.

These ideas are further explored in recent multiples such as *Cup & Saucer*, 2008, hand-painted bronzes beautifully presented in their own cases, which, while not prints, are a reminder that editioning is not the exclusive preserve of printmaking but a common practice within sculpture.

Bill Woodrow is a more idiosyncratic artist than Whiteread, whose sculptures bristle with inventive leaps of imagination, creating a world in which a discarded car bonnet provides the source for a camera and radio and an ironing board gives birth to an Indian headdress. He has produced numerous series of prints using predominantly etching and linocut which show how fundamental drawing is to his practice. These are prints that are directly made by the artist, alive to the relationship between tool and media, replacing the metal cutters and rivet gun used in making his sculpture with the linocut gouge and etching needle.

While the world's natural creatures are prominent in Bill Woodrow's work as in *Pond Life*, 2005 and *The Beekeeper Series*, 2000, for Roni Horn, it is the underlying forces of nature that provide her with inspiration. In the series of 15 lithographs, *Still Water (The River Thames, for Example)*, 1999, she explores the River Thames through photographs, which focus on the dark surface of the water, annotated with tiny numerals which reference footnotes in the border of the print. The footnotes refer to events and questions about the river, drawing the viewer in to a quasi-narrative "... and it turned out that the darkness of the river, which I thought was simply mud, etc., was in fact the darkness of London"[2]. The prints are dark, subdued and menacing, the surface of the water appearing alternatively like, oil or mud, its impenetrability heightened by the tiny numerals that further draw the viewers attention to the surface of the prints.

Text and image are likewise the signature elements in Hamish Fulton's work, which is sited in the concept of walking as a sculptural activity. His artworks, as with Richard Long, function to bring an essence of that experience into the gallery using words, lines and photography to create equivalents. He has used a variety of approaches as evidenced in *Porcupine*, 1982, made with Crown Point Press with soft ground etching, aquatint and photo-etching on three sheets of paper, to the more recent use of inkjet and vinyl texts stuck directly on to the gallery wall, taking the print into the realms of the mural.

RICHARD DEACON, *Show & Tell*, 1997.
C from a portfolio of 12 screenprints, 60 x 89.5 cm. Published by The Paragon Press, London, 1997. Image courtesy The Paragon Press, London.

RICHARD DEACON, *Show & Tell*, 1997.
G from a portfolio of 12 screenprints, 60 x 89.5 cm. Published by The Paragon Press, London, 1997. Image courtesy The Paragon Press, London. © Richard Deacon

RICHARD DEACON, *Show & Tell*, 1997.
/ from a portfolio of 12 screenprints, 89.5 x 60 cm. Published by The Paragon Press, London, 1997. Image courtesy The Paragon Press, London. © Richard Deacon

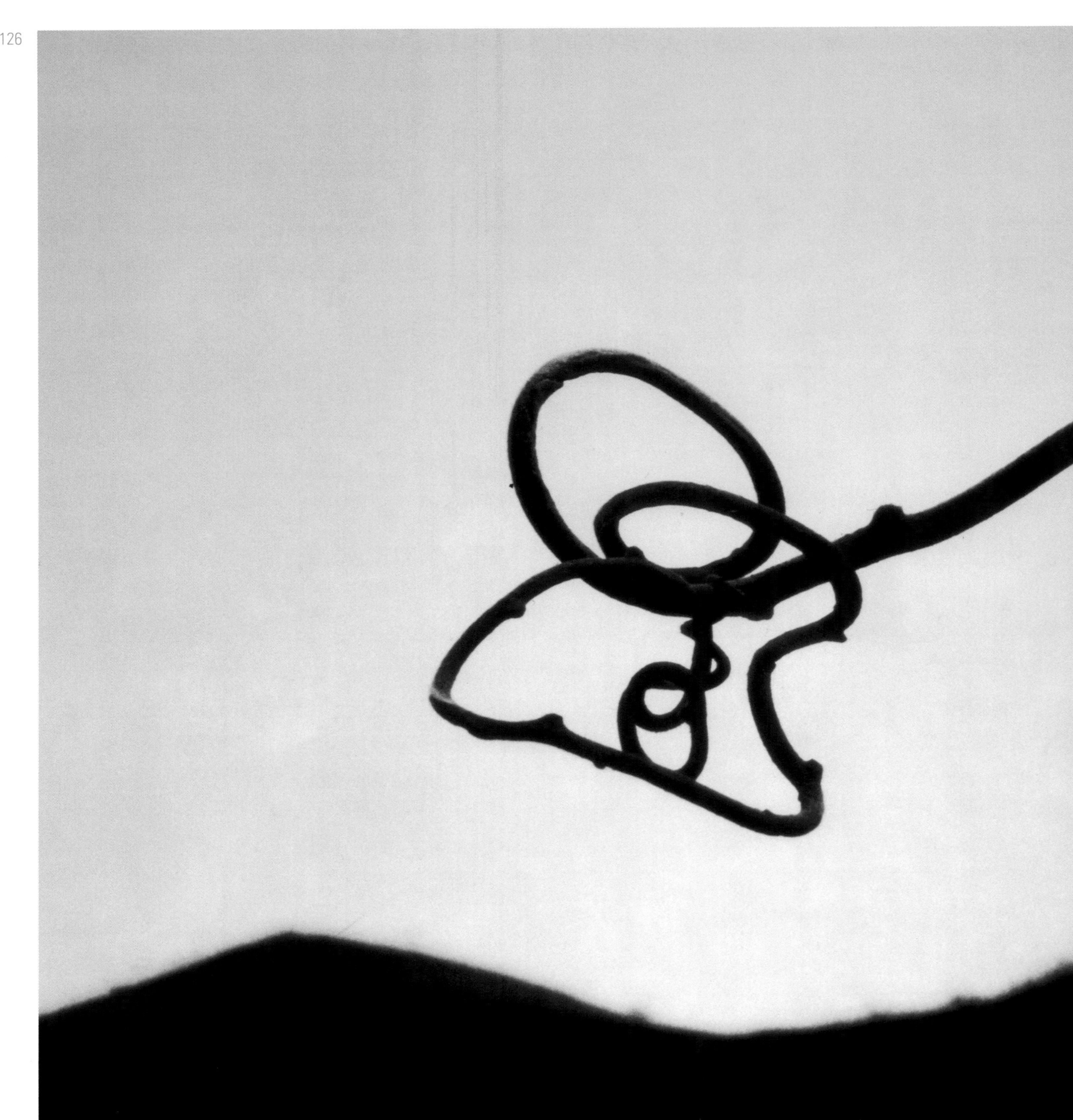

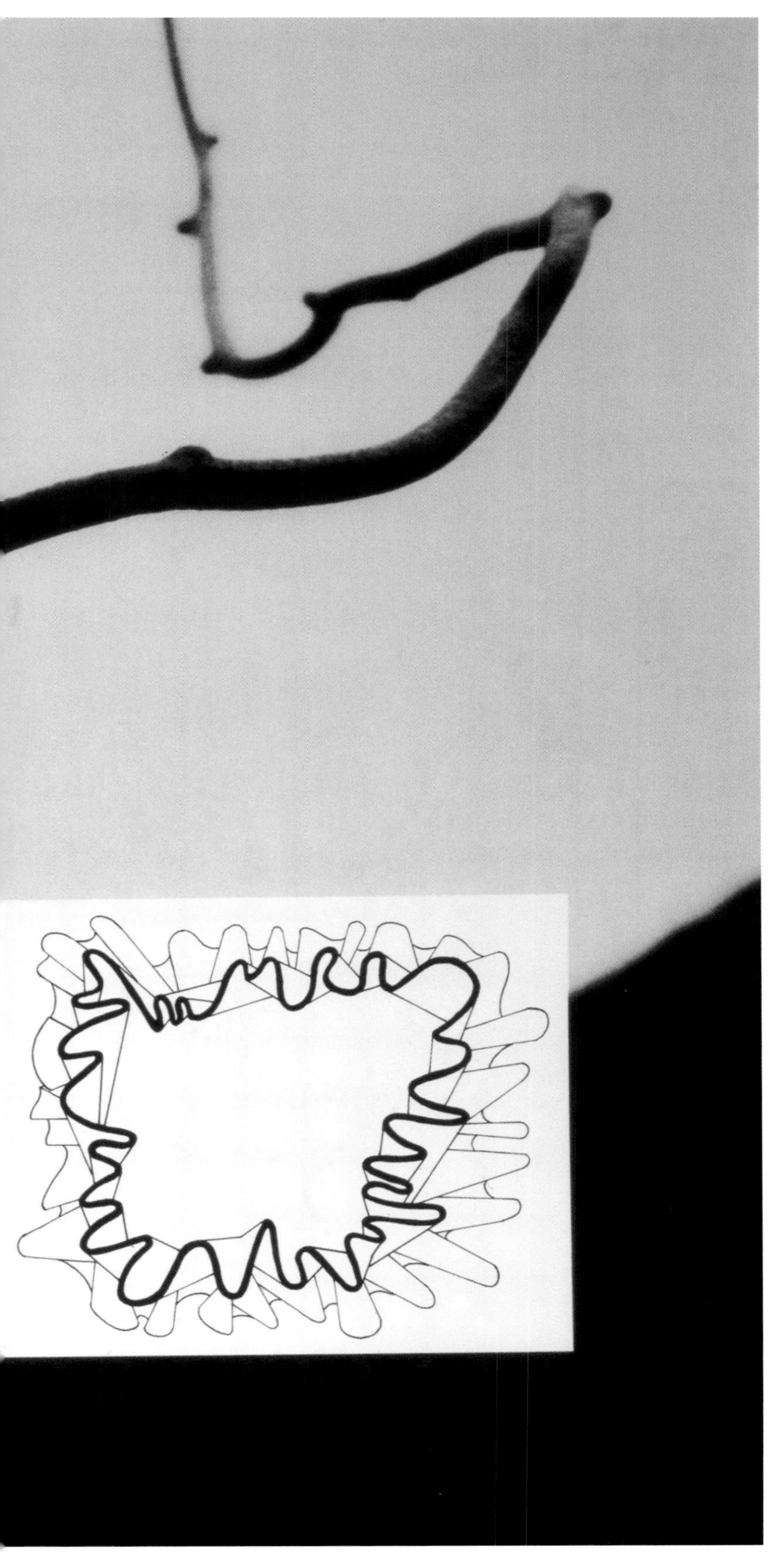

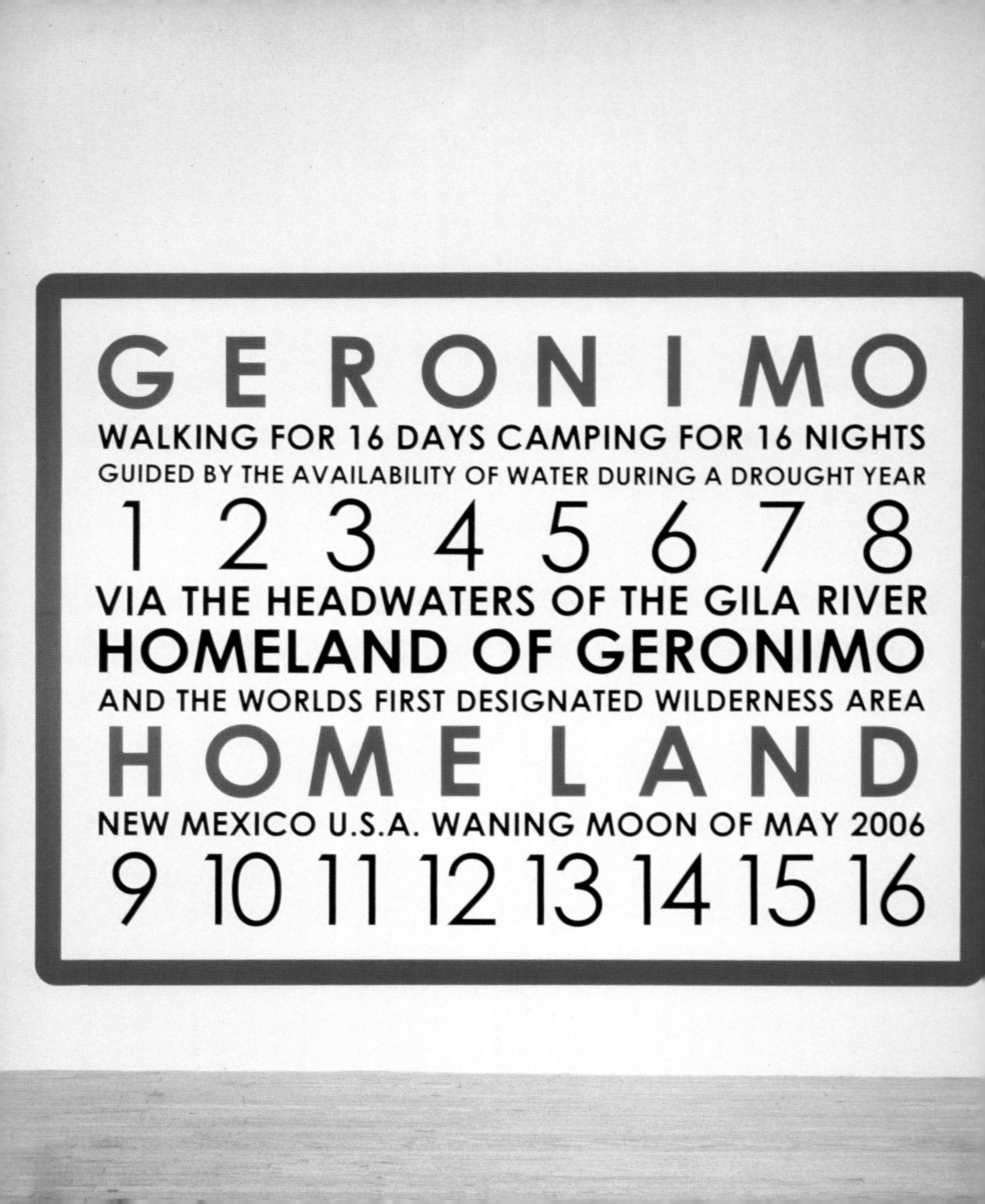

GERONIMO
WALKING FOR 16 DAYS CAMPING FOR 16 NIGHTS
GUIDED BY THE AVAILABILITY OF WATER DURING A DROUGHT YEAR
1 2 3 4 5 6 7 8
VIA THE HEADWATERS OF THE GILA RIVER
HOMELAND OF GERONIMO
AND THE WORLDS FIRST DESIGNATED WILDERNESS AREA
HOMELAND
NEW MEXICO U.S.A. WANING MOON OF MAY 2006
9 10 11 12 13 14 15 16

opposite: HAMISH FULTON, *Geronimo Homeland*, 2006.
Vinyl wall text, dimensions variable (As installed: 256.5 x 335 cm). Image courtesy of Texas Gallery. © Hamish Fulton,

below: HAMISH FULTON, *Porcupine*, 1982.
Colour soft ground etching with aquatint and photo-etching on three sheets of paper, 239 x 60 cm, edition of 25. Published by Crown Point Press, San Francisco. Image courtesy of Crown Point Press, San Francisco. © Hamish Fulton.

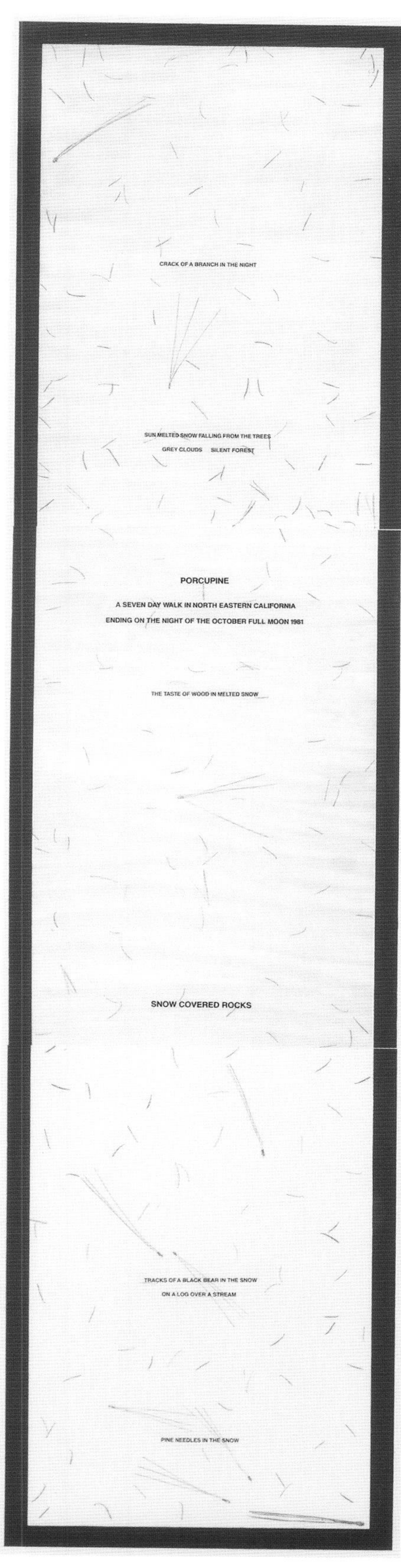

Whilst Fulton's work resides within a romantic idea of landscape, for the Irish sculptor Kathy Prendergast, the map itself has been a source to interrogate place. Attracting international recognition for her series *City Drawings*, 1997, working at the University of the Arts London, she made *Lost Map*, 1999, using the computer data for a map of North America. In collaboration with George Whale, the research assistant to the project, she was able to firstly remove all the place names that appeared on the map and then replace them with place names with the suffix "Lost". Each name was placed on its coordinates and gradually what emerged was an emotional map of North America composed of lost lakes, lost canyons and lost creeks. It was as if this hidden emotional seam, invisible on conventional maps, was exposed through the making of this work. "The map is an expression of the landscape but over and above that, it is an expression of us on the landscape. People have named all those places and what it's really about is the human condition. It's about our place in the world."[3]

The final print was printed as inkjet, resembling at first glance an ordinary map. Whilst this work could seem far removed from her very tactile sculptural practice, it is directly in keeping with her method of building up a sculpture or drawing from small, often repetitious actions, such as knitting or sewing, and through this heightening our sense of the interconnectedness of lives and experience.

While for the sculptors already mentioned, the activities of printmaking and sculpture remain distinct, for Christoph Loos it is an integrated practice. He works from tree trunks from which very thin sheets of wood, like veneer, are peeled off, providing a surface which in due course will function like paper to be printed on. The remaining trunk, now reduced, is then carved and in so doing, forms a cylindrical printing block which can be used to print on to the peeled wood leafs. As Loos states "All I need for my woodcuts is included in the tree. A closed system."

In the resulting installations, the printed wood and the block confront and reflect upon each other. "This synthesis draws on both the processes of relief printing and sculptural production and is characterised by a certain ambivalence and shifting between these classic genres, a result of the artist's activities as both a printmaker and sculptor."[4]

Sculpture and printmaking become inseparable in these works and act as a reminder of the shared concerns between these two disciplines both in terms of their materiality and in the manner in which the materials themselves are manipulated and are the subject of transformation.

KATHY PRENDERGAST, *Lost*, 1999.
Digital print, 85 x 132 cm. Courtesy the artist.

KATHY PRENDERGAST, *Mount Fuji with Cherry Blossom*, 2009.
Inkjet, 78 x 65 cm. Courtesy Kathy Prendergast and Kerlin Gallery.

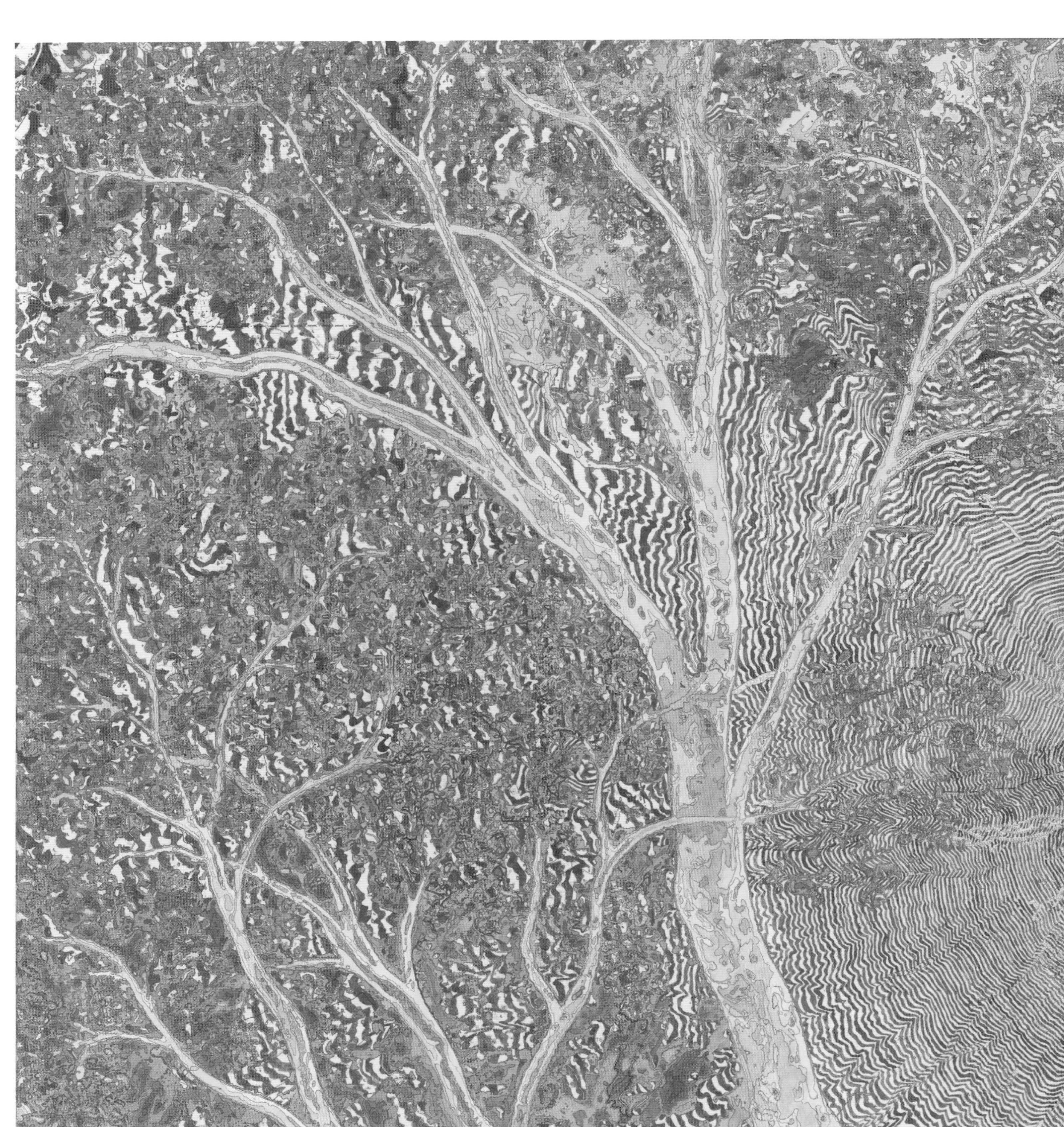

KATHY PRENDERGAST, *Mount Fuji*, 2009.
Inkjet, 78 x 65 cm. Courtesy Kathy Prendergast and Kerlin Gallery.

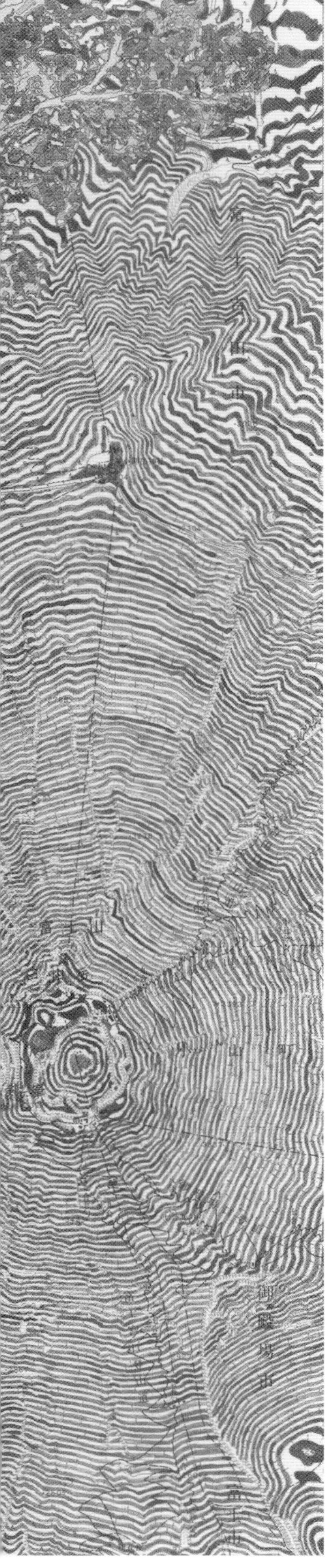

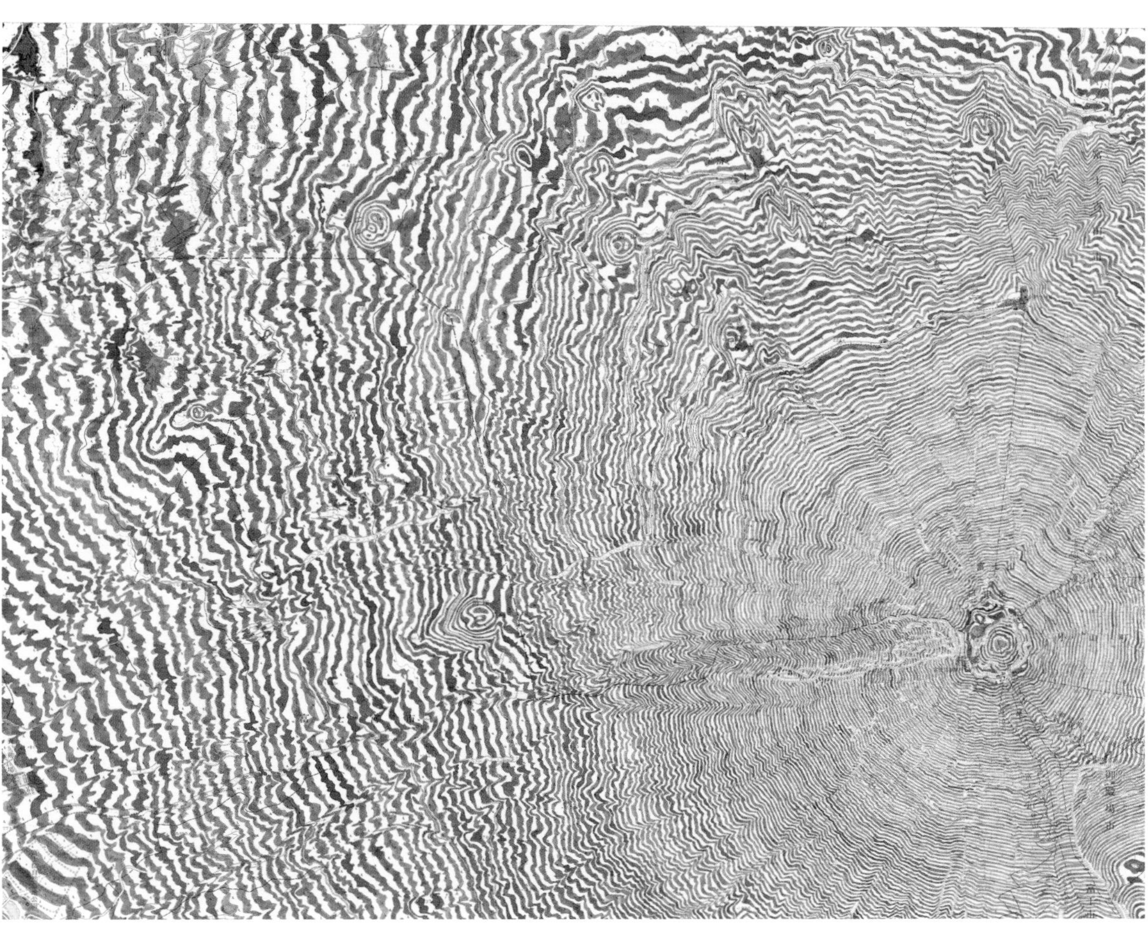

left: CHRISTOPH LOOS, *Time to be out of joint (I)*, 1995.
Woodcut on aspen sheet, 300 x 400 cm. Courtesy the artist.
right: CHRISTOPH LOOS, *Time to be out of joint (II)*, 1995.
Woodcut on aspen sheet, 300 x 400 cm. Courtesy the artist.

opposite: CHRISTOPH LOOS, *Time to be out of joint (III)*, 1995.
Woodcut on aspen sheet with printing blocks, installation. Courtesy the artist.

EXPANDE

NORMAN ACKROYD, *Windermere in Winter*, for Great Portland Estates, AFR Architects and International Art Consultants, Wells Street, London W1, 2008.
Etching on stainless steel, 300 x 275 cm. Courtesy the artist.

D PRINT

Andy Warhol's silkscreened *Cow Wallpaper*, 1966, or his printed *Brillo Boxes*, 1964, were an early indication that artists would look beyond the conventions of the framed limited edition print. For a number of artists, printmaking has been a means to work on installations as well as external architectural projects. The British artist Helen Chadwick used photography and printmaking extensively throughout her career, cut short by her sudden death in 1996. In the installation, *The Oval Court*, 1984, she took the most everyday form of printmaking, the office photocopier, as the means through which to create a mystical landscape of herself naked with other creatures, such as a swan and lamb. Appearing like a map of the constellations, these photocopies form a collage across the floor, on to which five golden spheres rest. It is a challenging piece not only in the way the artist exposes herself, but in the use of print, with scant regard for its conventions or longevity.

Bartolomeu dos Santos brought his extensive experience of etching to bear on a number of public commissions. Working in an experimental way, dos Santos created huge public murals etched in limestone for, amongst other sites, the Lisbon Metro. This experimental process gave him the fluidity to work directly on to stone with the same freedom as working on his etching plates. After etching, ink would then be rubbed into the stone as if ready to print. Oona Grimes, an artist herself and one of the assistants to dos Santos on this project, described the process as being very physical, with the stones first covered with an acid resistant varnish into which the image was drawn and "scraped into it with large scrapers and various sharp things". The etching itself was administered from watering cans filled with almost neat nitric acid, poured directly on to the stones and washed off with more watering cans filled with water. The process was completed by removing the acid resist with solvents and then rubbing ink mixed with hardeners into the etched surfaces to reveal the drawing.

Norman Ackroyd, a printmaker normally associated with atmospheric landscapes has produced a number of commissioned works for public places. In these pieces, he takes advantage of the graphic nature of the etched metal itself, using either stainless steel or bronze to fix an image of work within an architectural setting. This has resulted in architectural features including doors and balconies as well as large murals, as in a recent commission for the British Embassy in Moscow.

NORMAN ACKROYD, *Tempall Bheanáin—from The Aran Islands*, 2001.
Etching, 18 x 35 cm. Courtesy the artist.

BARTOLOMEU DOS SANTOS, *Library*, 1991.
Etching in limestone, detail of a wall panel in Entre Campos Station in the Lisbon Metro. Photo by Arnato Sousa. Courtesy Metropolitano de Lisboa EP and the Bartolomeu dos Santos Estate.

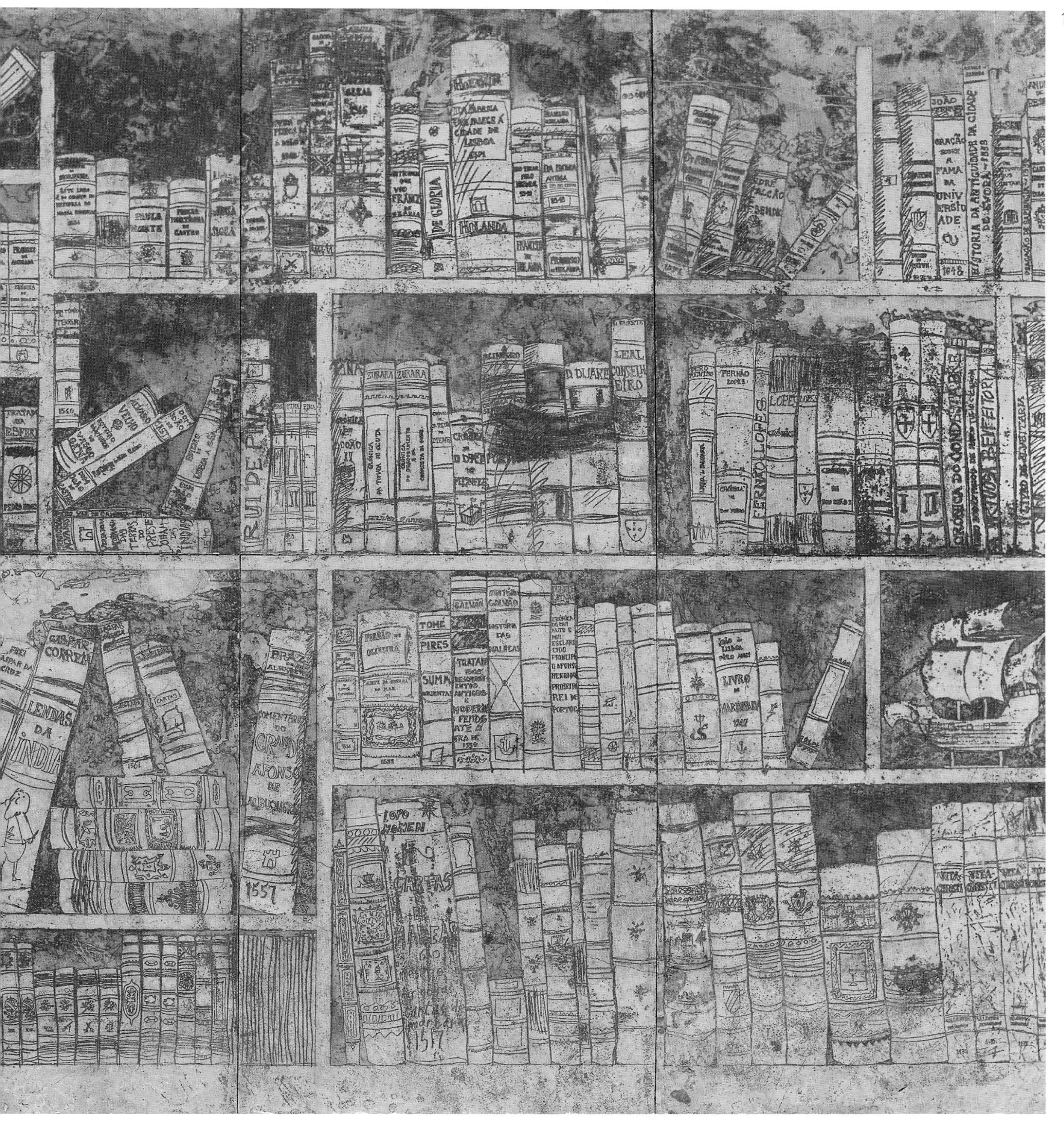
HOLANDA
DE GLORIA
ZURARA
ZURARA
PINA
D. DUARTE
LEAL CONSELHEIRO
RUI DE PINA
FERNÃO LOPES
LOPES
CRÓNICA DO CONDESTABRE
GALVÃO
TOMÉ PIRES
SUMA ORIENTAL
LIVRO DE MARINHARIA
CASPAR CORREIA
LENDAS DA INDIA
COMENTÁRIOS DO GRANDE AFONSO DE ALBUQUERQUE
1557
LOPO HOMEN
CARTAS
1517

THOMAS KILPPER, *State of Control*, 2009.
Lino floor-cutting, installation, Berlin 2009—former "Stasi-Ministry" (Ministry for State Security of the GDR). Photo by Jens Ziehe. Courtesy Neuer Berliner Kunstverein, nbk.

THOMAS KILPPER, *State of Control*, 2009.
Lino floor-cutting, detail, Berlin 2009—former "Stasi-Ministry" (Ministry for State Security of the GDR). Photo by Jens Ziehe. Courtesy Neuer Berliner Kunstverein, nbk.

Thomas Kilpper is likewise not confined by the accepted conventions of the framed print. As mentioned in the "Introduction", when presented with an opportunity to work in a condemned office block in South London, he used the parquet flooring as the woodblock into which he worked with routers and other tools. In a dramatic reversal, the artist used the floor as both the studio and the matrix. The imagery was inspired by the history of the site, an eighteenth century chapel that became in the early twentieth century a famous venue for boxing. In 2000, over the course of nearly six months, Kilpper lived and worked on the tenth floor of this building, Orbit House, methodically cutting his images directly into the parquet floor, using hand rubbing and a custom-built garden roller to print up the images.

The result was not only the biggest woodcut in the world, covering some 400 square metres when hung from the outside of the building, but also an installation inside, with individual prints suspended from lines across the room like washing. To further compound the transgressive nature of the work, the private view was staged on the very floor from which the prints were made. His most recent project, *State of Control*, 2009, has involved carving an enormous linocut from the floor of the former Ministry for State Security (Stasi), in Berlin. In conversation with José Roca, Kilpper reflects:

> It was the first time I made a large-scale linocut. The carving and cutting is very different. The ones done on wood have been much harder—you need a beater or toggle to carve, and wood splits off when the chisel is hammered in; it calls more for hard black-and-white contrasts. Linoleum is less resistant and softer, but does not jump or split away. It lends itself better to create grey tones and details.[1]

These linocuts, drawn from photographs, begin to suggest the secretive and menacing role of the Stasi, and how buildings themselves can be seen to hold keys to unlocking memory.

Fang Lijun, also draws on history, in his case, Chinese history, for the subject matter in his giant woodcuts. Whether depicting crowds of bald headed figures as in *1999.6.1*, or a head either drowning or swimming in *2003.3.1*, these woodcuts are built up from multiple printings of grey ink on to paper and fabric scrolls. In contrast to Kilpper, they are works of the imagination, born out of the events in the Tiananmen Square protests of 1989 and suggestive of a dark undercurrent of anxiety. Their scale is such that viewing these works, especially *2003.3.1*, covering as it does over 30 square metres, becomes in itself an immersive experience, the image dissolved into an abstraction as the viewer approaches.

The Brazilian artist, Regina Silveira also challenges our notions of what printmaking can be, working on a range of scales from the intimate through to large mural works. Working digitally and using laser-cut vinyl, she produced *Irruption: Saga*, 2006, a mural covering some 1,400 square metres, applied to the external architecture of the Taipei Fine Arts Museum, Taiwan, depicting hundreds of footprints. In another installation *Desapariencia (Taller)*, 2004, this time an interior mural, she translates a projected drawing of easels covering both the wall and the floor of the Sala de Arte, Publico Siqueiros in Mexico, disorientating the viewer and creating a collision between the illusion of the linear drawing and the reality of the space itself.

FANG LIJUN, *1999.6.1*, 1999.
Woodcut, 488 x 732 cm. The Museum of Modern Art. Courtesy Alexander Ochs Galleries Berlin I Beijing.

會

opposite: REGINA SILVEIRA, *Irruption Series (Saga)*, 2006.
Adhesive vinyl, approximatetly 1500 m². Taipei Biennial, Taipei Fine Arts Museum, Taiwan. Courtesy the artist.

below: REGINA SILVEIRA, *Desapariencia (Taller)*, 2004.
Adhesive vinyl, 236 m². El Cubo, SAPS—Sala de Arte. Publico Siqueiros, Cidade do México, México. Courtesy the artist.

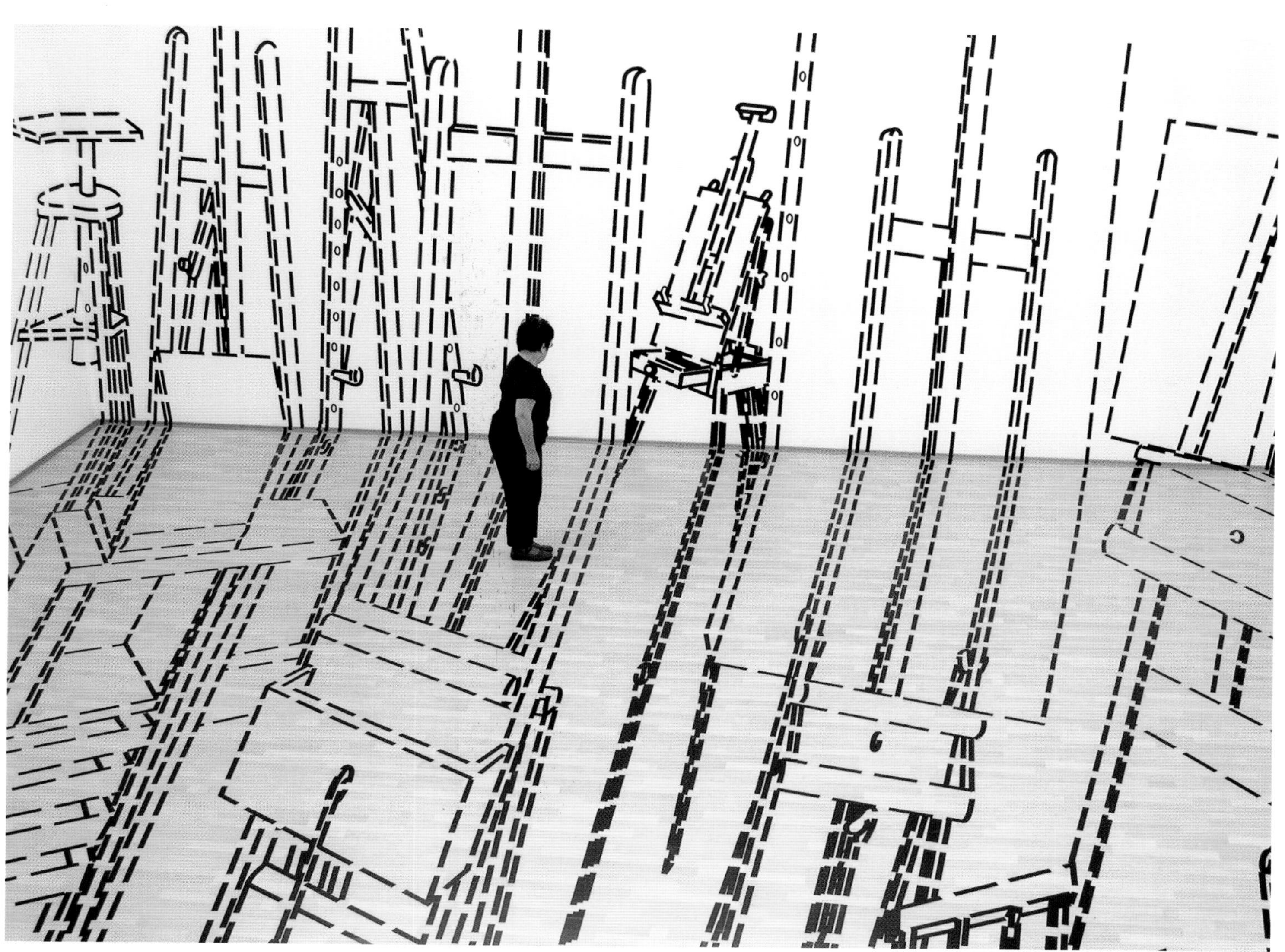

MICHAEL CRAIG-MARTIN, *Eye test*, 2005.
Duratran transparency mounted into lightbox, 128 x 61 x 3 cm, edition of 15. Printed at Omnicolour, London. Published by Alan Cristea Gallery, London. Courtesy Michael Craig-Martin and Alan Cristea Gallery, London.

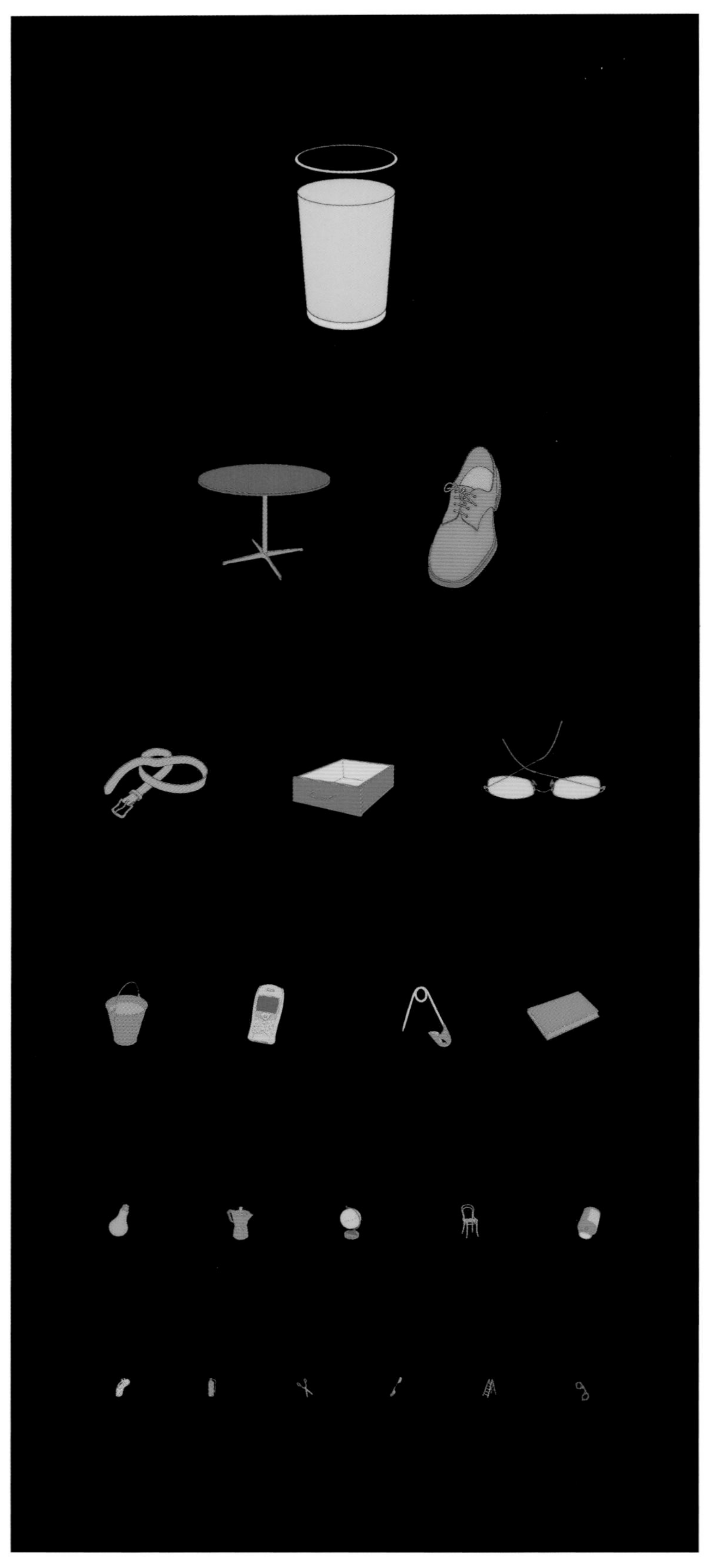

For Michael Craig-Martin, installation has been a prominent aspect of his practice since his early wall drawings in the late 1970s. His engagement with digital technology has enabled him to develop vector based drawings into a wide range of outputs, extending the language of printmaking. The definition of print becomes further blurred since it is within the computer that all the images are developed before resolving them through silkscreen, inkjet, installation or even as monitor based work. This variety of outputs can be seen in works such as *Becoming*, 2003, a computer and LCD unit with bespoke software that continuously changes a composition of vector drawings or in *Eye Test*, 2005, a beautifully simple proposition, a lightbox as one would find in an opticians, with, instead of letters, his familiar drawings in diminishing scale.

> I'm interested in objectness, physicality and the look of the world. I do have an interest in the ordinary but it's not so different to anyone else's, and I'm not really interested in consumerism or design. But I am really interested in language and the way these nameable objects are the basis of our language.[2]

In *Tokyo Sunsets*, 2008, Craig-Martin takes the technique of the rainbow roll, a means of printing a gradation of colours in a single pass of the roller or squeegee, and using inkjet, reworks this digitally, presenting six separate rows of prints depicting objects against an intense spectrum of colour. The complete work, measuring almost 2.5 metres in height locks the prints together as a singular object. His prints also become part of the very surface of the gallery, digitally printing the wallpaper for his large scale installations as in his exhibition *Surfacing* in 2004 at the Milton Keynes Gallery.

Richard Woods also plays with the contrast between illusion and reality, in his case, using plywood or MDF to make blocks from which he then prints on to thin sheets of MDF. These then serve as the material to either veneer furniture, clad a building or install as a new floor. Woods plays with languages of depiction, using stylised conventions to makes graphic representations of surfaces, for example, floor boards or bricks. He uses the signs for these materials in much the same way as a cartoonist would, and indeed there is a strong element of humour that permeates all these works. On one level they serve as striking visual jokes, such as *NewBUILD*, 2005, in which the fourteenth century Long Room in New College, Oxford, is dramatically transformed into a red brick terrace. There is an obvious irony that an Oxford College steeped in traditions of 'town and gown' is reinvented as red brick, the sign of the new universities. Furthermore, this transformation is so obviously insensitive to its location that he challenges that particularly English obsession with restoration, good taste and the preservation of heritage. Likewise, in his series *Logos*, 2000–2008, in which he installs brightly coloured graphically drawn printed floorboards, he taps into the current fashion of 'the makeover' and desire for immediate overall solutions and effects. In a further irony, since so many floor coverings are now made with laminate printed surfaces representing wood grain or marble aiming at a true and faithful representation, Woods in his garish use of colour and graphic rendition of planks, highlights this world of imitation.

Barthélémy Toguo is an artist for whom travel has both informed and shaped his practice. Toguo was born and raised in Cameroon before moving to Europe and now lives and works between Paris, New York, Bandjoun and Cameroon. In a remarkable work, *The New World Climax*, 2000, Toguo brought together sculpture, installation, performance and printmaking. Taking as a starting point the numerous stamps on his passport, he made large wooden 'rubber stamps' on to which he carved the words from the stamps on the endgrain, "Passport", "Number of Entries", "No issue", "Type of Visa", etc.. These then provided the blocks to print the work which fills the walls of the gallery, whilst the wooden stamps are displayed on large wooden tables. The words on the prints themselves are roughly carved, with no attempt to replicate the type, but they are given an 'official' quality through the endgrain itself revealing the structure of the wood in impressions which resemble giant fingerprints. This metaphor between the passport stamp and the most basic form of identifying the individual, the fingerprint, charges this work with deep and complex associations as John Peffer writes:

> If we return to where we began, to the *carte de séjour*, we see that Toguo is critically aware of both the illusoriness of the dream of fulfilment in the European "center" and the very real rewards that await those African citizens who successfully navigate the system and find a place for themselves there. Seen in this light, Toguo's rubber stamp, turned into a crafty piece of African wood sculpture, registers on several levels at once. It decries the prejudicial international system of border controls, which perpetually casts the (black) African as suspicious and potentially criminal, as opposed to the hardworking idealistic *émigré* he or she is likely to be. It also plays both sides of a popular (and itself quite naive) Eurocentric cultural bias according to which what is real and authentic in Africa and its diaspora is always going to be visionary, primitive, made by hand, and easily portable.[3]

A more lyrical approach to the idea of journey can be found in the print installations of Valgerdur Hauksdóttir. Her intention to "create a dimension between different realities of transparency and substance. A work that focuses on the energy of life, the connection between opposites, between exterior and interior" is manifested through a multimedia approach involving etching, lithography, collage, handmade paper, painting and sound.[4] In *Euphony*, 2003, the installation is a collaboration with the composer Richard Cornell, the sound is brought into play alongside the visual elements.

> There is no front or back of each work; instead the various pieces create an interplay of form, light and shadow.... Sounds and whispers of words in different languages are part of the installation....The sound is composed in random patterns so that at times the words can be distinguished from other environmental sound but often become a composition interwoven with the visual aspects of the work.[5]

The work evokes landscape with changing vistas and new sets of relationships as the viewer moves through the installation. Hauksdóttir's work points to the way in which print can be used as an element in a wider scheme, not for itself in isolation, but as an aspect of the artist's visual armoury.

MICHAEL CRAIG-MARTIN, *Deconstructing Seurat (blue)*, 2004.
A pair of screenprints on Somerset Satin 410 gsm paper, paper and image 63 x 93.5 cm (each sheet), edition of 40. Printed and proofed at Advanced Graphics, London. Published by Alan Cristea Gallery, Courtesy Michael Craig-Martin and Alan Cristea Gallery, London.

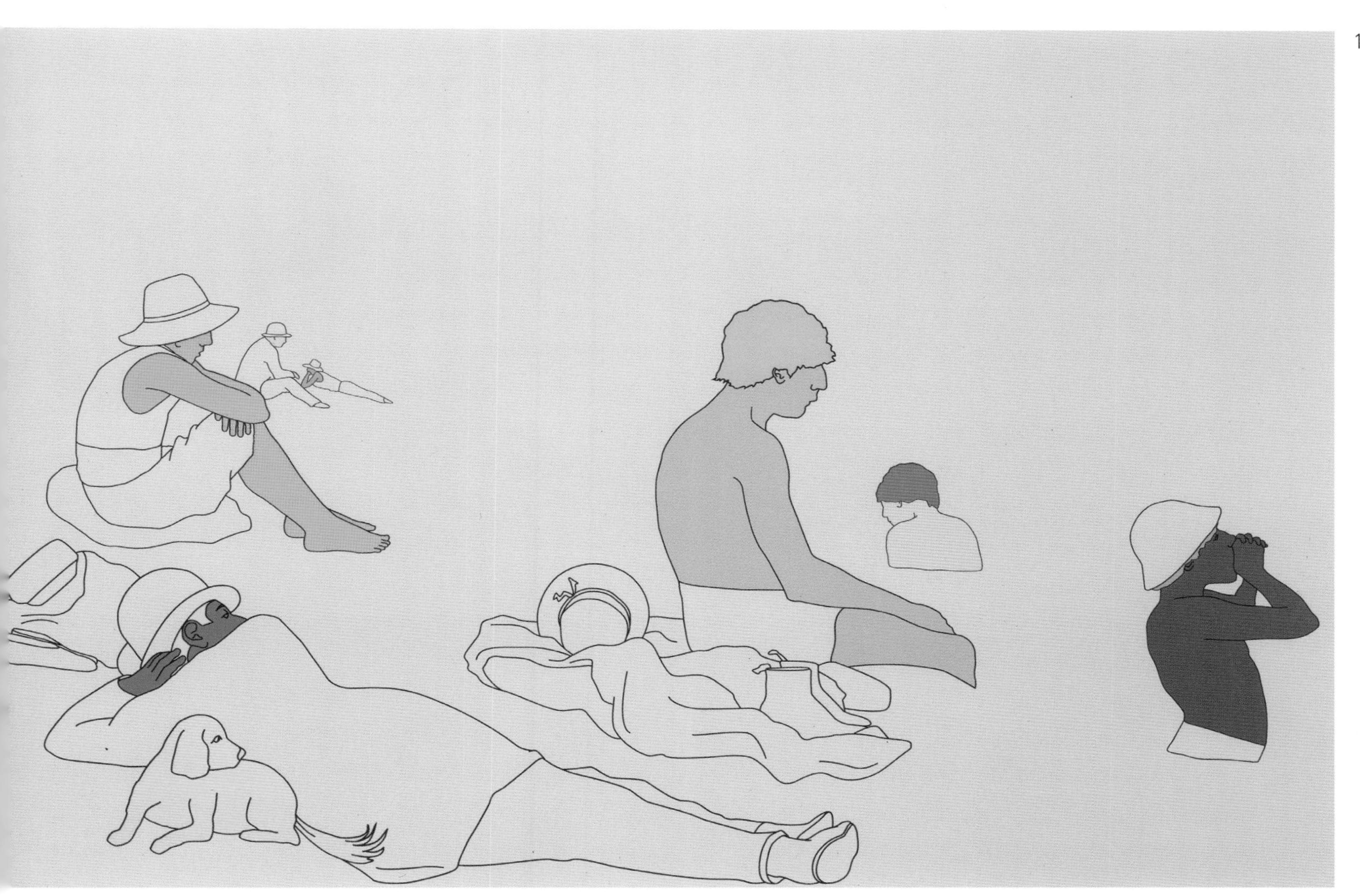

opposite: RICHARD WOODS, *Logo no.58*, 2008.
Installation view, A Colour Box, Arcade, London. Courtesy of Arcade, London. © Richard Woods.

below: RICHARD WOODS, *NewBUILD*, 2005.
New College Oxford. Courtesy of Arcade, London. © Richard Woods.

BARTHÉLÉMY TOGUO, *The new world climax*, 2001.
Installation, Art unlimited, Art Basel, Bâle, Switzerland. Courtesy the artist.

BARTHÉLÉMY TOGUO, *The new world climax*, 2000.
Woodcut blocks, 80 x 100 cm. Courtesy the artist.

VALGERDUR HAUKSDÓTTIR, *Euphony*, 2003.
Mixed media prints (lithography, etching, collage, painting), installation consisting of 16 prints on both sides of the paper, includes sound in cooperation with composer Richard Cornell, 240 x 20 cm, 240 x 55 cm, 240 x 90 cm. Courtesy the artist.

NEW TECH
NEW OPPORT

NOLOGY

UNITIES

Digital technology has resulted in both highly original works conceived and made within a new technical landscape as well as offering new approaches to previous printmaking processes. Examples to be considered include Julian Opie and Michael Craig-Martin's vector drawings which are used as the basis for screenprints and other works; Terry Winters' digitally cut woodcuts, through to Marilène Oliver's sculptural works, the result of scanned data. Other examples include Devorah Sperber who maps out pixels of Old Masters to be reconstituted through viewing the image in acrylic spheres and Susan Collins' seascapes, the record of the transmitted image, pixel by pixel over a period of 24 hours.

The vector line, drawn on the computer screen has presented Opie with a multitude of graphic possibilities, which have resulted in works ranging from screenprints, objects, films, screen-based works and even vinyl cut murals. Whereas in previous print technologies the image was physically linked to the matrix, for example, the etching being a mirrored reversal of the plate itself, new technology allows for a wide range of outputs from a set of given data. As a consequence of these possibilities, it questions the traditional definition of what might be regarded as a print. Opie's work has pushed at this boundary of what constitutes an original print, while also more broadly, at the intersection between disciplines, such as painting, sculpture and film. Throughout he has sought a reductive graphic language, providing the viewer with the very minimum of visual clues or signs necessary.

> The computer began to assume a central role in Opie's practice: it allowed him to develop his systems in abstract space before realising them in actuality. His key concepts were unchanged: the balancing of the generic and the specific, pitting realism against representation, and the working through of serial forms. Computer technology enabled Opie to develop new subjects whilst simultaneously expanding and refining his symbolic vocabulary to a degree of perfection.[1]

In recent years movement has been a recurring theme, as in the series of screenprints of a pole-dancing figure, *This is Shahnoza in 3 parts 05*, 2008, or the lenticular print, *Suzanne Walking*, 2005, through to animations, which are presented in the gallery on plasma screens with bespoke software.

Dan Hays has also become involved in the way in which the computer engenders new ways of seeing, particularly through focusing on the pixel and the reduction of information through low-resolution imagining. Whilst Opie has used lenticulars to explore the movement of bodies, walking, dancing, etc., Hays has engaged with the technology as a way of developing prints of wooded landscapes, that draw upon a history of the relationship between the mark and perception. Made with the FADE (Fine Art Digital Environment) research project at the University of the Arts London, these prints have developed from paintings derived from low-resolution jpegs and a continuing fascination with the pixel as an equivalent to the pointillist brush mark.

> Low-quality digital photographs can be seen as proto-paintings, abstracting visual information, creating painterly effects several removes from the world. We can zoom into these images with a similar wonder to the experience of approaching the surface of a painting, seeing how the illusion is generated. The agent for this is noise, a product of chaos and chance; the anomalies of entropic disintegration through flawed or mediated reproduction.... The quasi-object nature of lenticulars forms an alternative medium to painting in the translation of visual information into the physical realm.[2]

These prints fully developed through the computer on screen, revisit lenticular technology (a process more associated with kitsch images and cheeky postcards than high art) and through the bringing together of old and new technologies, create works of great refinement and visual intelligence.

In 2005, for the 26th Ljubljana Biennial of Graphic Arts, curators from across the globe were asked to curate small exhibitions in response to the question, "What is graphic art today?" Marilyn Kushner, the then curator at the Brooklyn Museum, New York, exhibited three installations by Devorah Sperber, each installation made from coloured spools of thread which when viewed through a sphere in front of the work, revealed a pixelated image of a painting by Leonardo da Vinci.

> In terms of the medium of printmaking, we are, indeed in a watershed period. At the beginning of the twenty-first century computer technology is creating a revolution in mark-making and, by extension, other media as well. And digital technology seems to have revolutionised not only the field of printmaking, but also the way in which some artists are looking at the world.[3]

opposite: JULIAN OPIE, *Suzanne Walking*, 2005.
Lenticular acrylic presented in an aluminium frame designed by the artist, framed size 116 x 73 x 4 cm, edition of 50. Published by Alan Cristea Gallery, London. Courtesy Julian Opie and Alan Cristea, London.

below: JULIAN OPIE, *This is Shahnoza in 3 parts 05*, 2008.
Flocking on three acrylic panels, each panel separately presented in a sprayed matt black aluminium frame specified by the artist, overall size 93.5 x 148 x 4 cm, edition of 30. Published by Alan Cristea Gallery, London. Courtesy Julian Opie and Alan Cristea Gallery, London.

DAN HAYS, *Nuclear Winter*, 2009.
Archival inkjet print behind lenticular sheet, 30 x 40 cm. Courtesy the artist.

DAN HAYS, *Colorado Snow Drift*, 2009.
Inkjet print behind lenticular plastic sheet, 42 x 56 cm. Courtesy the artist.

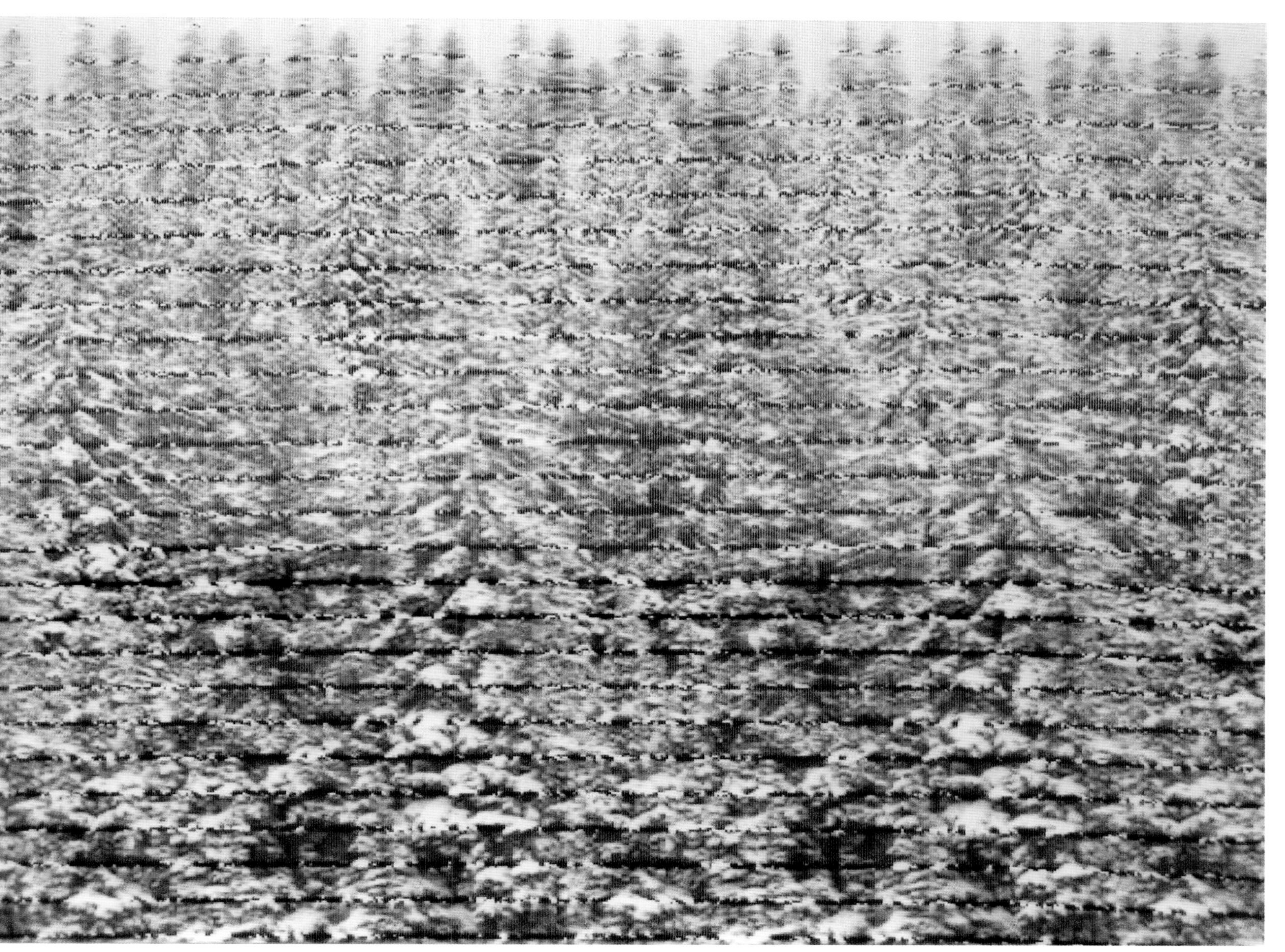

DEVORAH SPERBER, *After the Last Supper*, 2005.
20,736 spools of thread, aluminium ball chain, stainless steel hanging apparatus, clear acrylic viewing sphere, metal stand, 213 x 884 x 274 cm. Courtesy the artist.

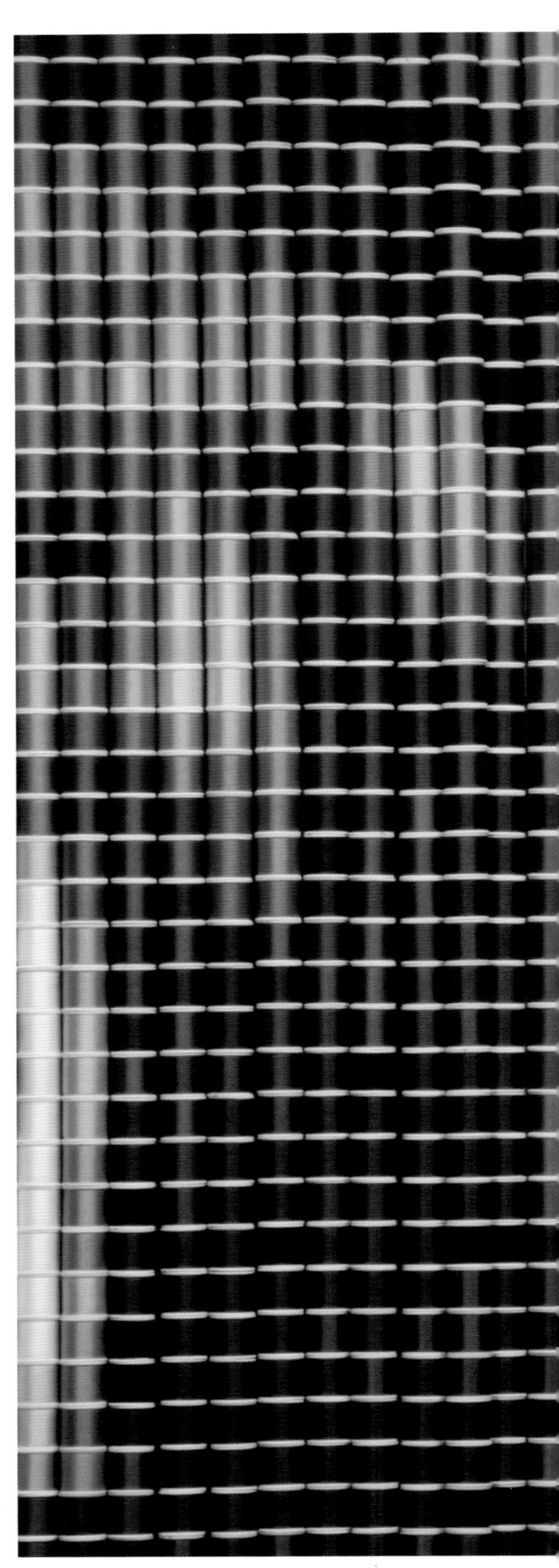

DEVORAH SPERBER, *After the Last Supper*, 2005.
20,736 spools of thread, aluminium ball chain, stainless steel hanging apparatus, clear acrylic viewing sphere, metal stand, 213 x 884 x 274 cm, detail. Courtesy the artist.

 Sperber, like Hays has engaged with the pixel as the unit of this new technology. Her installations begin "with computer prints, which she considers 'maps'. These maps pixelate the masterpieces and help Sperber determine how she will construct her works using spools of threads to replace the pixels on the two-dimensional maps."[4]

The spools, arranged according to her maps are colour equivalents of each pixel and these in turn are inverted and mirrored in the 'image' revealed in the acrylic sphere. Conceptually, this is so similar to traditional printmaking, with the artist pursuing a final image, through the manipulation of a matrix to a final goal that has a physicality in its own right. While it is perhaps speculative to describe the finished works as 'prints' the manner in which printmaking is embedded in these works, both practically as in the printed 'maps' and conceptually as in the transformation from the spools into a graphic image makes them particularly relevant in considering the initial question of what graphic art is today?

The manner in which the computer can be used to re-examine or offer new approaches to previous ways of working is also evident in Terry Winters' use of digitally controlled laser-cutting.

> As Winters has grown more involved with printmaking, he has expanded his practice to include intaglio, screenprint, linoleum cut, and woodcut. Additionally, he has experimented with new ways of using traditional print mediums. In *Graphic Primitives*, which demonstrates his interest in technology and cyberspace, Winters digitally manipulated drawings he had scanned into a computer before having them laser-cut into woodblocks. The blocks were then printed using a process pioneered by Pablo Picasso in which the blocks are printed in white ink before the sheet is rinsed in black ink.[5]

The bringing together of digital and physical technologies in this folio of prints offers compelling evidence of the way in which the computer can not only be a tool to develop and extend the artist's mark-making lexicon but can also sit alongside other tools to revitalise older established technologies.

The computer has also engendered a new relationship with the photograph, which once encoded, becomes as fluid a language as drawing. Darkroom techniques are now replicated through software and the digital photograph itself has become, for many artists, the replacement for the sketchbook with its capacity for instant referral. There is, of course, the danger that the artists vision become subsumed by technical possibilities and that the palette of filters in software programmes can produce work of familiarity rather than surprise. Therefore some of the more interesting work in this area employs the computer in rather a simple and direct way, retaining a feeling of urgency to realise the image.

Árpád Daradics, a Romanian artist now living and working in Hungary, has extensively used these new opportunities to develop a body of work, which takes old black and white photographs and brings them into a new existence by working with drawing on top of them. There is no attempt to disguise this layering of both time and technology, the added drawn elements sitting on the surface creating a sense of disquiet and imposing new meanings on to the original photograph. This is most famously apparent in his series, *Red Stories*, 2002, wherein one image, a photograph of the faces of three young men, are partially hidden by a lattice of red marks, in another, four men stripped to the waist are on fire. There is an implied sense of history and an intensity of emotion in these works, as he says, "objects, people, and ideas do not change over time, what changes is the way we see, observe, and understand them"[6].

opposite top: ÁRPÁD DARADICS, *Dance*, 2008.
Durst lambda print, photo paper, dibond, 80 x 60 cm. Courtesy the artist.
opposite bottom: ÁRPÁD DARADICS, *Popular fire*, 2002.
Durst lambda print, photo paper, dibond, 70 x 100 cm. Courtesy the artist

Top: ÁRPÁD DARADICS, *Masquerade*, 2005.
Durst lambda print, photo paper, dibond, 70 x 100 cm. Courtesy the artist.
Bottom: ÁRPÁD DARADICS, *Air raid*, 2003.
Durst lambda print, photo paper, dibond, 100 x 70 cm. Courtesy the artist.

TERRY WINTERS, *Graphics Primitives*, 1998.
Portfolio of nine woodcuts of Japanese Kochi paper, sheet 51 x 66 cm / plate 46 x 61 cm.
Image courtesy Matthew Marks Gallery, New York. © Terry Winters.

top: PAUL COLDWELL, *Sites of Memory-Book*, 2006.
Screenprint, 65 x 75 cm. © Paul Coldwell.
bottom: PAUL COLDWELL, *Sites of Memory-Suitcase*, 2006.
Screenprint, 65 x 75 cm. © Paul Coldwell.

PAUL COLDWELL, *Envelope/Crystal* from the series *Kafka's Doll*, 2007.
Inkjet with archival ink on Epson Stylus Pro 4800, 42 x 50 cm. © Paul Coldwell.

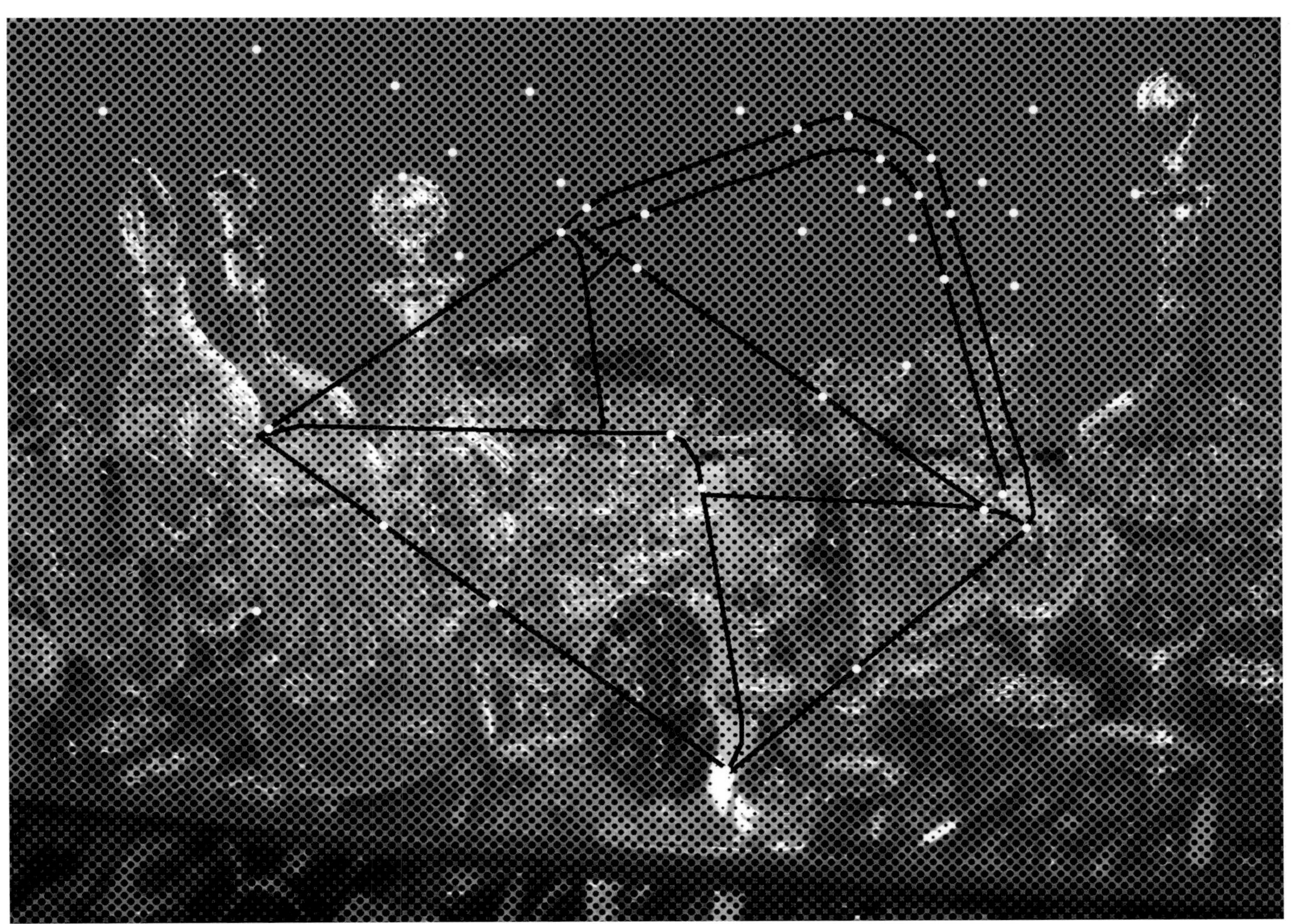

In my own work, the capacity for the computer to bring together photography and drawing has provided a rich vein for exploration. The screen has become the surface through which my prints are developed, leading to works which are either made as inkjet prints or as the means for making the layers for screenprint. In both instances, an aspect of my practice has been to proof continuously using inkjet to establish, right from the outset, the physical dimensions of the work, so that while the image is worked on screen, the reference is always to the proof with a fixed size and scale. In *Sites of Memory*, 2006, a series of screenprints, each layer was made in Photoshop with the photographic sources half-toned. Whilst in analogue darkroom processes, the half-tone would be a fixed set of relationships; using the computer, each dot could be modified, literally drawing the half-tone. The imagery for these prints reflect an ongoing concern with ideas of journey and loss and the manner in which objects of familiar things might suggest aspects of a life.

The narrative that is embedded in my own work is replaced by a systemic, almost scientific approach by the artist and filmmaker, Susan Collins. In recent years she has been using web cam technology to provide live streaming that record and picture landscapes, building up the images over time, pixel by pixel. Parallel to these film projects she has also made static images in the form of digital prints that take selected slices of time as a single image. At first glance, these prints of Collins' can seem like landscapes from a romantic tradition. Her recent series *Seascapes*, 2008, recording the view out to sea is reminiscent of Mark Rothko's late grey paintings. But on close inspection, the seascape is revealed as an image built up of individual pixels, each with a colour value, in parallel lines, starting at the top left hand corner and working across and down; the seascape is an accumulation of each of the pixels, transmitted over a period of time.

> The original web cam work was programmed to record images pixel by pixel, with a whole image representing approximately a day. Through the nature of low-resolution still capture and enlarged enormously, Susan's intention was to reveal a coding and decoding of the landscape. [...] it was fascinating to witness how the digital building blocks of the image were revealed creating beautiful abstracted passages through wholly unexpected combinations of coloured pixels.[7]

SUSAN COLLINS, *Seascape, Folkestone, 25th October 2008 at 11:41am*, 2008.
Digital inkjet print on Somerset photorag paper, 183 x 137 cm. Commissioned for Seascape by the De La Warr Pavilion, Bexhill-on-Sea and Film and Video Umbrella. Image courtesy the artist. © Susan Collins.

SUSAN COLLINS, *Seascape, Stokes Bay, 27th September 2008, 14:13pm*, 2008.
Digital inkjet print on Hahnemuhle photorag paper, 101.5 x 76 cm. Commissioned for Seascape by the De La Warr Pavilion, Bexhill-on-Sea and Film and Video Umbrella. Image courtesy the artist. © Susan Collins.

TIM HEAD, *Dust Flowers 1st Series*, 2006.
Digital inkjet print on Hahnemuhle 308 gsm photorag paper, 97.5 x 97.5 cm. Image courtesy the artist. © Tim Head.

In essence each work is a condensed movie, the result is an image of strange beauty, hovering between film, painting, photography and print. This preoccupation with the basic ingredients of the digital image is taken one stage further in recent prints made by Tim Head. Working with the programmer Eli Zafran, Head uses the individual inkjet dots as his building blocks for these abstract works;

> By operating at the primary scale of the medium's smallest visual element (the pixel or, in this case, the inkjet dot) and by treating each element as a separate individual entity the medium's conventional picture-making role is completely bypassed. The prints are no longer tied to the interpretation and reproduction of an external source (an image created on a screen) but become instead the direct embodiment of the printer's own intrinsic characteristics. You are no longer looking through the medium at a representation of an imported image but looking directly at the raw grain of the digital medium itself, the fine dust of the inkjet print. The medium is no longer transparent but opaque.[8]

Whilst the thinking behind these works reveals a cool rational approach, the resulting prints are luscious, intensely physical and painterly, the shimmering

TIM HEAD, *Dust Flowers 2nd Series*, 2009.
Digital inkjet print on Hahnemuhle 308 gsm photorag paper, 97.5 x 97.5 cm. Image courtesy the artist. © Tim Head.

of colour across the surface drawing the viewer in. Head describes these prints as providing "a counter to the overload of demanding images that are presented to us every second, 24 hours a day... an antidote to that... a brief pause".[9]

Marilène Oliver draws upon the medical use of digital imagining for her pieces that take printmaking through to sculptural works, installations and commissions for public spaces. For Oliver, digital technology not only provides the process of making but also through the internet, her source material. She is intrigued by "how the machine looks at the body".[10] Through accessing medical imaging data (MRI scans) on line, Oliver is able to manipulate the data in order to construct her 'figures'. Her first work using this process took scanned images from the internet of a convicted murderer which she selectively screenprinted on to 90 sheets of acrylic which were then stacked to form a three-dimensional print, an apparition, a ghostly image of the deceased. Her work has since developed to include works which use Computed Tomography (CT) data sets as source material and how the re-arranging of an axis can transform the image. She has also realised works through digitally engraved acrylic sheets as in *Exhausted Figure*, 2007, or in using printed colour, as in *Heart Axis*, 2007.

MARILÈNE OLIVER, *Heart Axis*, 2007.
UV cured inkjet and optichromic and interference ink (silkscreened) on to polycarbonate, acrylic stand, 162 x 117 x 75 cm. Courtesy the artist.

MARILÈNE OLIVER, *Exhausted Figure*, 2007.
Engraved acrylic and fishing wire, 170 x 55 x 35 cm. Courtesy the artist.

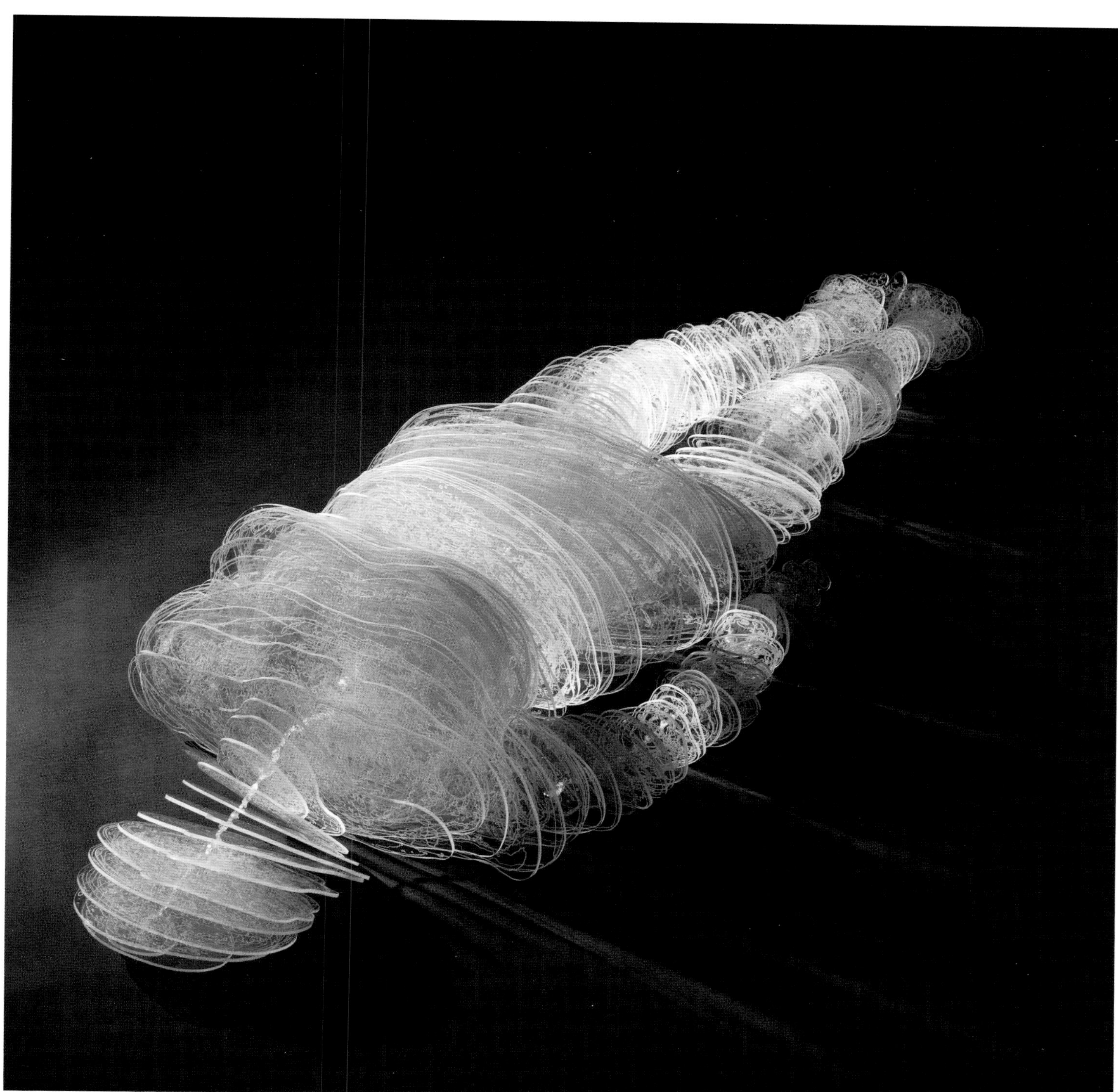

CÉCILE BOUCHER, *Back and Forth*, 2006.
Digital print, 150 x 70 cm. Courtesy the artist.

The portrait as opposed to the body as a whole is the subject of scrutiny in Cécile Boucher's digital prints, *Back & Forth*, 2006. The central motif is the head seen from the back, concealing the owner's identity. In the surrounding space, tiny rectangles are scattered, revealing themselves to be fragments of the person's face. In her own words, Boucher states that:

> They show photographs of the backs of the heads of different persons, surrounded by much smaller, pixel-like squares that seem to have escaped from the central image. The smaller squares are like pixels in that they contain both a part and the totality of the information for an image which, upon close inspection, turns out to be the face and the identity of each individual.[11]

These works, hung as groups, play with the notion of scale that the computer has engendered, the act of zooming in and out of images and the resulting sense of dislocation between the whole and the parts. Boucher's work takes these propositions into the space of the gallery and into the work's physical interaction with the audience. Whilst the singular images of the backs of heads, presented life size, can be read from a distance, the viewer is inextricably drawn to the surface, the tiny fragments of information demanding a close inspection. Paradoxically, the viewer then becomes an element in the work, pressed against the surface, his or her own head now both configuring and obscuring. For all the information set into these prints, 300 individual photographs in each, one is still presented with a mystery and an overwhelming sense of alienation.

In contrast to Oliver's and Boucher's focus on the body, Marko Blažo, a young Czech artist, draws reference from the imagination, derived from amongst other things, computer games and invented spaces. His work appears formed by rules that he then takes great delight in breaking, visual puns and graphic invention abound, recalling in style the work of the abstract painter, Al Held. Blažo's prints are marked by their energy and strident flat colour, recognisable elements such as houses and hearts seem to be linked together by dynamic networks of lines like electric circuits or architects' diagrams. These works hover between the languages of graphic design and fine art, demonstrating the rich interplay and crossover between these disciplines and the manner in which the web is used as both a source and medium.

For many of the artists mentioned, the use of the computer has been a development out of and building upon traditional practice. Increasingly, however, we will see a younger generation, brought up with this technology for whom the sharing of images and their role in social networks may well be more important than locating the practice within a tradition of printmaking. The definition of printmaking will need to change to accommodate these developments as increasingly the boundaries between disciplines blur and the nature of art practice changes in response to technological advances.

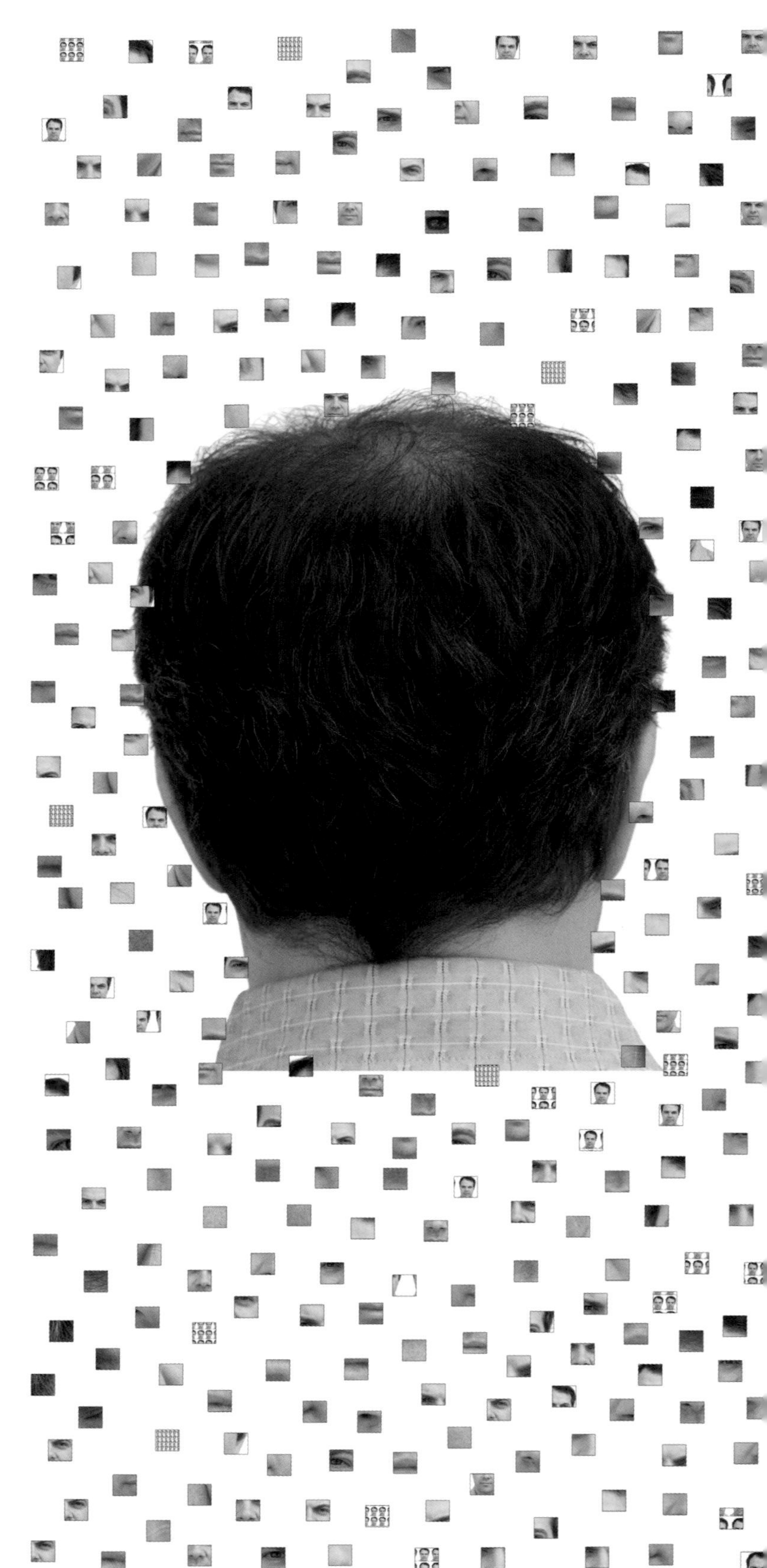

MARKO BLAŽO, *Seven Complexes*, 2008.
Digital print, 60 x 90 cm, paper 75 x 105 cm. Courtesy the artist.

MARKO BLAŽO, *Butterfly from Beijing*, 2008.
Digital print, paper 100 x 145 cm / image 90 x 135 cm. Courtesy the artist.